LANDFALL 245

May 2023

Editor Lynley Edmeades

Reviews Editor David Eggleton

Founding Editor Charles Brasch (1909–1973)

Cover: Gavin Hipkins, *Five Lemons*, archival pigment print, 480 x 600mm.

Published with the assistance of Creative New Zealand.

OTAGO UNIVERSITY PRESS

CONTENTS

4	Charles Brasch Young Writers' Essay Competition 2023 Judge's Report, *Lynley Edmeades*
6	Muscle Memory, *Xiaole Zhan*
10	Treatment Plan, *Evangeline Riddiford Graham*
12	Hypothetical, *Evangeline Riddiford Graham*
14	The Edge of the Sea, or Sea Rose (1977), *Jodie Dalgleish*
16	Louise's Sea, *Jodie Dalgleish*
17	The Beautiful Afternoon, *Airini Beautrais*
22	Men_u, *Nafanua Purcell Kersel*
24	Rātapu/Aso Sā, *Nafanua Purcell Kersel*
26	A Jar, *Nicholas Wright*
27	The Monarch Without, *Nicholas Wright*
28	Sixteen Ways to Incite a Revolution, *Maria McMillan*
34	ACC Lullaby, *Liz Breslin*
35	Letter to the Editor, *Medb Charleton*
36	In Search Of, *Medb Charleton*
37	No Good, *Ruben Mita*
39	Stare Down the Sea, *Lisa Onland*
45	Swimming to Australia, *Tim Grgec*
47	Midnight Tea, *Tim Grgec*
49	The Garden Tour, *Annabelle O'Meara*
51	Caselberg House, Broad Bay, *Tim Upperton*
52	Heaven's Suburbs, *Mark Edgecombe*
54	We didn't notice when the trees along the boundary line went missing, *Zoë Meager*
56	the indefinite article, *Brett Cross*
58	The Moth-eyed Steeplechase Horse, *Emma Neale*
60	A Name to Remember, *James Pasley*
67	Invocation, *Gregory O'Brien*
69	Such is the way with dreams, Simon, *Jackie Davis*
71	Dualism, *Philip Armstrong*
72	black druid, *Philip Armstrong*
73	View to the Alps, *Michael Mintrom*
74	Sound Waves from the Lost Planet, *Michael Mintrom*
76	Flowers, *Holly Best*
81	Drowning the Children, *Shirley Eng*
83	Ci serve un titolo (Settler Vectors), *Lorenz Pöschl*
85	18 sex treats, *Janet Charman*
88	ART PORTFOLIO, *Gavin Hipkins*
97	Another Poem with a Found Feather, *Nick Ascroft*

98   The Thing Is, *Claire Orchard*
99   White Noise, *Rachael Taylor*
107   I said *greyhound, Rebecca Ball*
108   That Silver Sea, *Rebecca Ball*
116   Transmutations, *Nicola Thorstensen*
117   Stung, *Cindy Botha*
118   if a star explodes on a distant ceiling who will see the light, *Rachel Smith*
119   Kō, *Derek Schulz*
120   Buy Now, Pay Later, *Derek Schulz*
121   A Quidam, *Steven Toussaint*
122   An American, *Steven Toussaint*
123   Overhaul, *Josiah Morgan*
124   Heart of Gold, *Phoebe Wright*
130   White Irises, *Brett Reid*
131   Within the Room, *Jennifer Compton*
132   Te Hau o te Atua/The Breath of Heaven, *Kerrin P. Sharpe*
136   Singapore, *Lincoln Jaques*
137   The Father, *Jackson McCarthy*
138   Der Rosenkavalier, *Jackson McCarthy*
139   Love Was Not on the Programme, *Alexandra Fraser*
140   Pursuit, *Danielle Heyhoe*
147   Bird Life, *Bill Nelson*
148   Near Things, *Brent Kininmont*
152   ART PORTFOLIO, *Anya Sinclair*
161   Afloat (Our Daily Bread), *Ahimsa Timoteo Bodhrán*
163   bleak time, *Amber French*
164   Mr Andrew King, *Paula King*
165   Living and Company, *Jonny Edwards*

THE LANDFALL REVIEW

172 Landfall Review Online: Books recently reviewed / 173 CHRIS ELSE on *The Axeman's Carnival* by Catherine Chidgey / 176 JENNY POWELL on *Winter Time* by Laurence Fearnley / 179 SALLY BLUNDELL on *Making Space: A history of New Zealand women in architecture* edited by Elizabeth Cox / 183 EMMA GATTEY on *My American Chair* by Elizabeth Smither; *Renoir's Bicycle: A collection of prose poems* by Michael Harlow / 188 NICHOLAS REID on *Voices from the New Zealand Wars | He Reo nō ngā Pakanga o Aotearoa* by Vincent O'Malley / 191 DAVID EGGLETON on *Out of the Jaws of Wesley: 1944–1972 a record: Peter Olds* selected and edited by Roger Hicken

202   CONTRIBUTORS
208   LANDFALL BACKPAGE, *Amanda Shanley*

LYNLEY EDMEADES

Charles Brasch Young Writers' Essay Competition 2023 Judge's Report

Standing in a gallery in Mumbai many years ago, my travelling companion said she thought that looking at a piece of art was like having a silent conversation with an artist. The conversation is one-sided, of course, but in reading and looking we have access to conversations that transcends the boundaries of time and space. That piece of art we were looking at in Mumbai was a portal to a world—*someone's* world—that I never would have had access to otherwise.

Other people's worlds are endlessly fascinating. And yet, some are more accessible than others (indeed, some voices are more accessible than they deserve to be). Reading these essays by young writers from across Aotearoa, I felt like I'd been given access to the private lives of those I'd never normally be privy to, like they'd openly shared their concerns and vulnerabilities. But they're not shying away from the big stuff: social justice, climate change, sexuality, gender, mental illness, the cost of living, the place of history, the pitfalls of social media. I was reassured by the domination of political themes in this year's entries—at a time when futility prevails, these writers are actively engaged in thinking about how we might make this world a better place, even when it's obvious—to them and us—that it's not their fault the world is so messed up.

And yet, to write about the big issues is one thing; to craft these issues into a lyrical and sophisticated essay is another. What placed the winning essay head and shoulders above the rest in this year's competition was how carefully and innovatively formed it was. 'Muscle Memory' by Xiaole Zhan begins with a small vignette about dissecting a dead sheep while attending a high school science camp, and ends with a meditation on gender, language, and the body. In between these two rather disparate poles, it meanders through a performance of Macbeth, reflects on learning to play the cello, the experience of singing in a choir, thinking through the Renaissance idea of women's bodies as 'leaky vessels' alongside John Berger's conception of looking; it contemplates systems of oppression, personal pronouns, antidepressants, and much more. As a kind of instantiation of the leaky body, the shape of the essay itself refuses to fit into neat paragraphs; the writer lets each thought leak from one paragraph to the next, refusing punctuation and easy containment. This refusal is also largely what 'Muscle Memory' is about: being 'misgendered and forcibly defined by the violence of a colonial language' and finding a language that is, like music, more fluid in its 'learning and adapting and destroying and creating.' This essay, like the body, like language, is sprawling and leaky. Insightful, lyrical and incredibly sophisticated, 'Muscle Memory' is an essay to be much admired.

The other essays I have selected were also engaged with big ideas, and each offered up its own idiosyncratic view of these issues. 'What Makes a Woman?' is almost a companion piece to this year's winning essay, concerned with categories of personhood and questioning the reductive binary of 'man' and 'woman'. Kay Stodart's essay draws heavily on Monique Wittig, the French philosopher who, in 1978, famously said 'lesbians are not women', drawing attention to the notion that to be 'woman', one must be reduced to a specific relationship to men, economically, politically and ideologically.

The two commended essays were both selected on the merit of their subject matter. 'The World is Calling to You, Answer' is essay-as-political-mobiliser, recalling the author's first public protest and the power and potency of collective political action. 'Notes on Androgyny' also joins the conversation of the two winning essays, and bravely comments on the lived experience of 'an androgynous cis woman' who doesn't necessarily identify as either category of 'woman' or 'queer'.

Congratulations to all these young writers. Thank you for these conversations. I implore you to keep writing about this stuff; we have much to learn.

Winner: 'Muscle Memory' by **Xiaole Zhan**
Second place: 'What Makes a Woman?' by **Kay Stodart**
Commended: 'The World is Calling to You, Answer' by **Isabelle Lloydd**; 'Notes on Androgyny' by **Phoebe Robertson**

XIAOLE ZHAN

Muscle Memory

I am seventeen with naked knees hacking into the trachea of a dead sheep. The smell will stain me, like bloodshot snow, or the taste of cigarettes and alcohol from somebody's lips the night before on my toothbrush in the morning. I am one of the teenagers on a science camp in a white laboratory at Auckland University. I am dissecting a pluck—the heart, trachea and lungs of a carcass. The noun 'pluck' is derived from the act of plucking the viscera from a body after it is killed. It makes sense to me—I think of the gut strings of baroque instruments, cords prepared from the walls of intestines. I think of what it means to play a passage in pizzicato; to pluck the string. I begin to dissect the heart, approximating the lines of the left ventricle, scissoring through the discoloured fat. I breathe through my teeth, my head spinning. I am

there again, fifteen, a groundling at the Pop-up Globe. I am looking up into the stage lights at Lady MacBeth's hands, blood-splattered. My vision narrows, my breathing is shallow. Half-conscious, I stumble past bodies onto the wet grass outside. I am drowning; the horizon is at my throat. My body wants me to escape but forgets that I can't escape my body. Somebody appears above me and I look up. I smile, sheepishly. Yeah, I'm fine. Oh, this happens at every show? Thanks, yeah, I'll take the sugar. My hands are pale as they unwrap the orange lozenge. The sweetness draws my body back toward myself. No, I didn't feel stressed at all. No, this hasn't happened to me before. I'm usually fine with seeing blood. It's like my body did its own thing, and I suddenly realised that I was seeing in tunnel vision. It's like I sometimes

see myself beside myself, as if I'm not entirely a part of my body. As if I could approximate my own heart apart from myself, the size of a fist hovering from an arm that happens to belong to me. When I was fourteen, I started learning to play the cello. Playing never became easy for me. Every movement was body-heavy; each note carried with it the abdomen, the back, the shoulders, the length of the arm, the joints of each finger. The curve of the wooden body bit into my sternum and thighs, leaving red rashes. In the winter, my fingers stung with blisters oozing yellow pus. The blisters hardened into calluses, which I would bite off mindlessly when I was anxious. The shape that music takes within the body is different for every instrument. Sometimes I close my eyes and I can

feel the music in my hands. The curve of a palm against somebody's forehead becomes an open fifth upon the piano. The opening E minor chord of the Elgar Cello Concerto stings against the pointer finger of the left hand. Learning music made me realise that I am not a genius of the body. Musicality and physicality are one and the same muscle. Knowing how the music moves is not enough; you also have to know how to move the body in a way that follows. The genius of knowing one's body can be seen even in childhood; in the prodigy dancer, in the small fingers that find a home on a quarter-size violin. You can learn to sing before you learn to speak. Sometimes you need the ease and the instinct of

screaming. When I was sixteen, I sang in my high school choir. My high school singing teacher always told me I thought too much before opening my mouth. I could never find a way to release the nervousness from my tongue and my jaw and my shoulders. My singing teacher told me that sometimes you must stop thinking altogether and trust what the body knows. He said that singing is just controlled screaming. I didn't know until then that what happened in my mind would also bury itself in the tightness of my throat and the lump of my tongue. I remember singing Bruckner's motet, *Os Justi*, as one of the first altos in the choir. The psalm is sung in Latin—the line, *Lex Dei ejus in corde ipsius*, translates into, The law of his God is in his heart. I learnt then that corde in Latin means both string and heart. The chordae tendineae, the connective tendons in the anatomy of a heart, are more commonly called the heartstrings. Every time the choir reached Bruckner's repetition of the phrase, *in corde, corde, corde*, I couldn't help but begin to weep, secretly, in the tightness at the back of my throat so that I couldn't continue to sing at all. My body betrays me again and again as a musician. My piano teacher joked in my first year of university that my unconscious movements at the keyboard made him seasick. I want to save the tears for the audience, but sometimes I can't control my own body's screaming. Tears, milk and blood—the emission of these fluids from the body led writers in the Renaissance to refer to women as 'leaky vessels'. When I was nineteen, I read about how a woman's self is split in two. She watches herself being watched; is at once the surveyor and the surveyed. I don't remember if it seemed strange to me at the time for John Berger to write so authoritatively about being seen as a woman from his vantage point as a man seeing women. *The surveyor of woman in herself is male: the surveyed female.* What happens when women see

each other? When one isn't entirely at home with the way their body is seen? When I was twenty, I realised that my body had always been symbolic against my will. The body cannot escape language as language cannot escape the body. We are lily-livered, cold-hearted, wrong-footed, hard-nosed, hawk-eyed, and ask day after day if we can offer each other a hand. When I looked at myself, all I could see was a collection of limbs articulated by a language that didn't belong to me. My body would change and then change again and be claimed by words handed to me by the same culture that described bodies like mine as leaky vessels. When I was nineteen, I learnt that I had clinical depression. I stopped having my period for four months at a time due to physiological stress. When I started taking antidepressants, my body gained weight and my skin became covered with stretch marks like the lines left in sand by the tide. At twenty-one, I've stopped trying to escape my own body. I realise that bodies are fluid things that will keep on changing. The body

remembers, my high school counsellor told me. The body remembers the muscles it uses when you laugh so hard that your stomach hurts. You have to think of those muscles when you're performing those giddy staccatos, my singing teacher told me. You have to imagine the sound keeps travelling even after your hand presses the key that moves the hammer that hits the string, my piano teacher told me. You have to imagine your bowing arm is like a pair of lungs helping you to breathe, my cello teacher told me. The body has to remember because the problem with music is that it disappears. I'm not sure where the music goes once the hands leave the keys. I'm not sure what it is that strings one second to the next second, on and on. I think a melody is the strangest thing—a row of ghosts holding hands across

the death of each second. At twenty-one, I've gotten used to slipping in and out of existence. Sometimes I feel like I'm dragging the weight of a body that belongs more to the continuation of systems of oppression than to myself as a person in my own right. Sometimes I'm just too tired to assert the existence of my body. *Why do you want to make things difficult for yourself? Isn't the world already too divided? Why do you want to go on creating yet another category?* My friend's uncle grills them with these questions at a family wedding. I think of the boys' school across the road that changed the pronouns of a love song so it wouldn't be gay. *Why do you want to make things difficult for yourself?* Sometimes I just want to leave the supermarket with my groceries, or agree with strangers so that I can step off the tram at the next stop and walk home. I am misgendered and forcibly defined by the violence of a colonial language more often than I am recognised on my own terms. There are moments, though, when I am surrounded by people who listen to the language I use for my body and speak it back to me. I am always articulating and rearticulating myself with a language that I'm still reaching compromises with—learning and adapting and destroying and creating. I think this articulation will change and change again as my body does. The body unfolds over time as music does. We need to be listening.

EVANGELINE RIDDIFORD GRAHAM

Treatment Plan

My sister thrust my head through the laurel.
'There,' she said. 'Now you smell like a victor.'

    Once I knew a boy named Victor with eyes

long as snow peas. But we were babies.
Inside me, the shadow moved but a little

    —merely there, trick of the light or active

only as a culture is in yoghurt.
'Your mother kept a biscuit by the bed,'

    my father reminisced. Twenty-five months

since she popped out for milk and cigarettes
and still he could not resist. I left

    a trail of brick, buddleia, wouldn't

touch a potato for the impression
of blood under my nails with each bite.

    My sister said, 'I'll buy it, just take the—'

I once loved Victor whose nose was wet.
Viewed from its interior, the laurel

      tree is private. Even there in the green-

dark atrium, with victory wreathed
across my eyes and quiet, I could not

      speak to my snow pea. It was evident

I had no plan for us: just the one name
I tested and left in the branches.

      There was a spider over my breast.

Raked the bush of its leaves on my way out.
'What an active fragrance,' I said, zesty

      and I'd actually lost weight. At the verge

my sister worried the grass. Everyone
made encouraging noises from the car.

      Like a winner I brandished the bay leaves,

tore a whole geometry from the main
and stuffed it in my handbag. For later,

      that is. I'm not saying it was a cure.

Hypothetical

Although they had not used the name as children, when all the women were grown there came a time when they referred to the man as Daddy. Daddy, they asked, have you been to the doctor yet? Did you buy her any birthday presents, Daddy?

There was something infectious about it and soon the man began calling himself Daddy.

Hello sweetheart, he would announce, strolling into a kitchen, Daddy went to the market and got you some nectarines.

It was all they had hoped for. Rather than holding himself apart, Daddy had reconciled. He was regal, teetering, generous. They were all very grateful. Daddy had not made a habit of history or genealogy. Daddy had a passion for Swedish cakes made of almonds and butter.

The women were lenient: if Daddy were malicious, to her especially, it was to be expected and it was only now and then. And if it were in some part true that to be called Daddy suddenly, and at a great age, was a kind of mockery—its dangled erotica trip-wired with incredulity—no one thought enough of that to say anything about it.

But the women had forgotten their mother, who sang out Daddy without irony or threat, like a girl on a gate calling out to her own father Daddy, Daddy!

Galled, the women locked their mother in the cupboard.

When Daddy came to their houses looking for her, the women said, Say Daddy, you have too many cares. Rest up and stay here a while.

To the women Daddy said, I will need a little pallet. And he went down to sleep very quietly.

The next day he said to the women, Now I will need a little chair and desk. He tinkered away at his chair and desk and when night fell he lay down to bed.

And in the morning Daddy said to the women, How about my breakfast?

JODIE DALGLEISH

The Edge of the Sea, or *Sea Rose* (1977)

For Joanna Margaret Paul, and i.m. Imogen Rose, Feb.–Dec. 1976

like this is her sweet, delicate presence in the dry stick of a room,
that's hung between heavy umber curtains, in the whiteness
of the table's vase that warps light like it's underwater, and holds
the pastels of ochre, blue, and a rare leafy green and grey, to
its flower that's so full and soft it's like the old breaking of a loaf
of bread, floured and fleshy, to a velvety wine, as its petals bloom
outwards to Carson's The Edge of the Sea: the sea rose that
arcs cup-like to each of its shores ('Rocky', 'Sandy', 'Coral'), that's
of the long rhythm of the sea that casts and recasts itself in the soil;

in a shoreline that binds them to the most basic, intimate mode of
circling to the same enquiry of how to draw a life, in its detail—
in the nearby Selliera radicans (perennial, succulent herb-creeper
with white half-star flowers), and its roundleaf, rotundifolia, version
(small distinctive orbiculate leaves trailing tidal streams), of the same
family as the wing-seeded mountainous version: as to why feeling
always exists on the verge of a body's classifications: as to what's
in the signal of hordes of diatoms that flash their microscopic lights
at night; or why wisps of transparent protoplasmic sea lace inhabit
a coast in their trillions; or the way a colony of hidden sea squirts
form themselves into easily visible flowerlike clusters;

its beat, ebbing and flowing along a course that's in the way words
probe and prove the porosity of the artist's picture of her daughter's
heart she had breaking from the newborn's forefinger in Imogen, the
way the daily membranous tissue of 'almost trivial roses' ran to the
palp and pulp of colour fleshed inside a heart, a sea rose, that a

beloved (inno) child (gen) sleeps into, here, like an ocean holds to
the diaphanous, slight movement of a language, rolling, rocked from
blüte (bloom) to bluten (bleed), the way her work circles the circle
of a working, beloved's, heart, sending its blood to the lungs.

Louise's Sea

After Louise Stevenson's Through the Middle of the Earth

If I make each stitch on this globe
    a circuit around a body of
wants, the way my body
    wants to take to the
water, the way I remember
    its deeper, darker blue
tied to an island of islands
    telling of what moves with, and past, us
as we journey on the rolling
    folds of its swell;
I'd string the best figuration
    of us to the ocean's
space for my care's reach,
    and we'd ride on
the way the ear's external 'pinna' (auricle)
    sends this same term for a flora's leaflets,
    named after the divisions of a fin, wing and feather,
breaking as 'pinnulate', in the edges of a tree fern,
sailing inwards, to where
    saying your name to such intricate designs
carries the same soft 'shush' as a swiftness that's like
the vertigo of a hemisphere fallen, threaded and blood red
through a needle's precise point for piercing paper;
for the continued coolness of what
    water brings, and what it pulls from me,
    to where you are.

AIRINI BEAUTRAIS

The Beautiful Afternoon

Beneath our feet the seafloor is hairy. We step through the fur of seaweed, out onto rocks, place foot after foot in the beautiful afternoon. We are emerging from the water, wet. Like life from the primordial soup. The sea has a damp organic smell. We come out of the brine, where sailboats tack, where swimmers push away from land. We emerge onto land again.

Sun warms the brown necks of beer bottles. I lend you my towel to dry yourself. Then we sit on it. It does not matter if the coloured diamonds on the towel are the wrong colours. It doesn't matter that my bikini is patterned with flamingos, or your shirt with words. It doesn't matter if we are clothed or unclothed. We are in our bodies, beside each other. It doesn't matter how many times we have seen each other's bodies before, or what our bodies have been to each other, or how. We have made this time. We sit on my towel, and there are flax bushes, and there are pōhutukawa trees, and there is grass, sharp and green. There are other people in and out of the water, but only you and me in the beautiful afternoon. It doesn't matter how we made it, what brought us here. Here we are.

'What is that bug?' you say, picking a small black creature off my leg, but I know the bug is not important, you just want to touch me. I want to touch you too. We hold each other, and kiss each other, as we have before, as if we never have before. Both our mouths taste of beer and of the sea: salt, minerals, organic matter. The sun is on the water. Around us there are harakeke bushes. I don't notice if anyone else passes us and sees us holding each other.

We walk along the beach. We talk about human bodies: not so much our own, but bodies in general. You are easy to talk to, although there are some subjects we have never broached. The beach is full of people, their bodies having been let out for a romp, for a few hours. So many bare bellies and limbs, all shapes and sizes, all ages. In the restaurant beside the beach people are eating and drinking. Some of this is pleasure, some of this is homeostasis.

Back at the beach house, we have sex. The sheets grow sweaty, sprinkled with sand. While we are having sex, we both say things we would never say in other circumstances. We say things that would make me laugh if I were not aroused. Then we lie in the warm air of the beautiful afternoon, in the beach-house bed where so many transient people have slept and wanked and fucked. The conversation is now mundane. We are talking about the plot of Star Wars when you lean over, mid-sentence, and we have sex again.

The beautiful afternoon is passing. The twilight is falling. The twilight here is also beautiful: I feel as though I could live in it. Not with you, but with the streets, the warm air, the subtropical gardens. I know I need to leave. Even if I could stay, I know I can't deal with a whole night of this, and breakfast. It is too much. You make me a cup of tea, then we get in the shower. All you have is some kind of three-in-one body wash, which you smear over me. 'You're going to smell like a dude,' you tell me, and I reply, 'There's probably worse things I could smell like.' The water runs over my head, through my hair, the bubbles of surfactant travel down to my feet and swirl down the plughole. Over and over, you run your hands down the length of my body, from my head to my toes. My body loves this: the repetition, the pressure on my skin. In this moment I feel like a statue of a goddess, something people might visit from time to time, leaving flowers or food at her feet. I feel like a statue that gives people things. You stand up and we kiss again. Our bodies would go another round but I need to get on the road. We turn off the water and step out into the generic white towels of the twilight.

I am a few blocks away when my phone rings on the passenger seat, your name on the screen. Are you going to ask me to stay? Would I? Are we going to talk about the things we never talk about? No—I have left my towel and bikini on the washing line. I get back to see you standing in the driveway, under the pōhutukawa trees, holding everything neatly folded. I race the sunset, drive to a basic campground in a park where my family used to go for big extended family picnics. I get there just as the pink goes from the sky and the gates are being locked for the night. I have a new tent unopened in its bag in the back of my car. In the last mid-grey of evening, I figure out how to put up the tent. Then it is completely dark. I make a cheese and tomato sandwich in the darkness, using the car boot as a table. It is a disgusting sandwich but I am so hungry I just eat it, with a cup of cold water. Then I unroll my bedroll and sleeping bag and go to bed. Kids are still up, playing spotlight around the campground, and some of them hide between my tent and my car. I don't care, I am so tired. I am so tired I don't even feel the sharp pain in my heart I normally feel when I hear the sound of other children playing and my own children are far away.

In the small hours I am woken by a voice calling 'Mama! Mama!' It goes on for a bit, then dies away. Then I am woken again by a very pronounced 'Quack!' as a duck walks by. I brush my teeth in the communal bathroom, alongside mothers brushing their children's teeth. I feel wrong and out of place. What am I doing here, a woman on her own, without her children? Why would a woman alone be camping here?

At your beach house you will be eating breakfast. I am not particularly thinking about you this morning. And, I imagine, vice versa. I go for a walk along the beach, through nīkau palms and over sand, feeling like I am in some faraway jungle. I am a secondary character in the story of your life and when I exit stage left, I no longer exist. I am not angry at you now. We had a beautiful afternoon. I am angry at you weeks, or months, or years later, for a raft of reasons. But it is not really anger at you, it is anger at myself. Or anger at structures. And then that too passes and there is nothing left of it. Like a table where food and drink are served and spilled and made a mess of; then the plates and glasses and cutlery are all cleared away and the table is wiped clean. Nothing suggests the meal that was had.

I pack up my tent and head off again. 'You're off, are you?' says one of the campground dads. We have a friendly conversation. The campground is full of mums and dads, throwing frisbees, hanging wet togs on tent ropes. They have remembered the gas stoves and the picnic blankets. They are all good at being families. Flame trees arch over the road out. I stop at Orewa for a coffee in an Italian café full of the elderly. There is a man at a table with four women. The ratios get like that, as people age. Are they a group of platonic friends or have they decided that as they are retired and have money, they will abandon societal norms? Do the women share the man among them? They all look happy, talking animatedly. How do we get old? How do we do it?

★

I am in Kawhia, spending a second night in my new tent. I have come here because I have never been here, and I have discovered that the main reason people come here is fishing. The village is a mix of fishing baches, run-down houses, overgrown sections, a couple of campgrounds. I am not here to fish, and my presence feels somehow inappropriate, like turning up at an event in the wrong kind of clothing. A toddler is fussing in the tent next door. His parents and grandparents are with him—he is a first baby, reassured from all sides. On the other side of me is lawn, then an insignificant fence between the campground and the neighbouring property. The campground's neighbours have a loud family fight, with lots of accusations and swearing, then a visitor drops by and the woman has a jovial, friendly conversation with him, as if nothing has happened. Maybe families just get into the habit of yelling and swearing when they are upset, and sometimes it's meaningless. And sometimes it's not.

It is kind of nice lying here in my tent, with the door open and the light deepening over the estuary. The water is metres away. Coastal reeds grow at its edge. I have the peace and quiet and rest I have craved. On the other hand it is lonely lying here, eavesdropping on other people, and I will probably drive home tomorrow. I am running out of enthusiasm. I take a photo of the view from my tent, but don't send it to anyone. The beautiful afternoon, which was yesterday, already feels like the distant past. I go for a run around the village. I have a shower. Children and their mothers cluster around the bathroom block and the trampolines. Again, everyone here is with family or friends. I am discovering why no one goes solo camping.

My children are on a two-week holiday with their father. I have made a brick path behind my garage, digging the sand, placing the bricks. I have tended to my plants. Reading *Spinster* by Kate Bolick, I decided to challenge myself to holiday alone. I packed a notebook and a pen, *Spinster*, and some other feminist books I got out of the Whanganui library. I am slowly making my way through the small feminism section. I have journeyed up through the middle of the fish then down one side. In Tokoroa I stopped at an op shop and found a book of Sandra Coney articles, *Out of the Frying Pan*. 'There is no longer a rigid life course for women consisting of school, work, marriage, motherhood and menopause,' Coney writes in her introduction.

'But many of the old issues remain for women and there are new ones.' It felt a little like the book had found me.

Darkness falls again. In the cabin behind my tent, a group of people are drinking. A young couple have returned from the harbour, where they crashed their jet-ski on a sandbar. The woman has injured her wrists in the impact but thinks the whole thing is hilarious. Her laughter encourages her partner, who tells the story multiple times, his drunk voice braying above everyone else's. Then he lapses into homophobic jokes. There is no one here I want to talk to, nowhere I can sit and drink companionably and feel content and safe. I lie in my tent, in my sleeping bag, hoping I have gone undetected, that no one will ask me who I am and what I am doing here.

In the morning I go to the communal kitchen, have a tin mug of black tea and a plastic bowl of muesli, wash my dishes when the sink is free. I have a brief conversation with some strangers about where I am from and where I am going. 'Oh, Whanganui, Whanganui's a great place,' one of them says. I am doing what I have always done when I am alone: latch on to any human connection, try to prolong it, to surround myself with it. Aloneness does not appeal to me at all.

I walk along the beach looking for the hot springs, but don't find them. I take the back roads through rural Taranaki, through hamlets I am too scared to stop in, where seagulls pick over rubbish piles, and men with wild hair sit on front porches staring. I am too scared even to park my car to eat lunch with the windows up and the doors locked. I eat at the wheel. I am not having fun any more. I am just tired, lonely and terrified of the things I have seen.

The road has narrowed right down. Native forest grows up steep hills on either side. Low over the road, a falcon swoops.

NAFANUA PURCELL KERSEL

Men_u

Breakfast at 9
a mean man delivers me from my fake broken earrings slipped off and i still have to go get four packets of smokes for aunty from the dairy so break me fast, beat my tiny armour wearing off on my arm bent back and i hope the money stays in my pocket with the slip of paper from aunty's hand, *rothmans 25s*, i hope i get her selau smokes back to the kitchen where she is baking a pie stuffed so full it breaks its own golden brown body and the gravy sneaks out to burn off until the pie is just pastry and dry meat, almost empty but still looks full

Lunch at 12
he's far from the farm i think, this kid in my class who has called me a bitch because i slapped him when really i wish i bit him is that what a bitch slap is not the slap but the person who owns the hand and uses it against his pocket-monied cheek for squeezing his chubby hands on my butt to check the dough while we were waiting in the tuckshop line and why am i even in trouble for this is it because the force of my slap was more than the force of his grip but my armour is the thing that clinks across the concrete floor

Drinks at 18
drown years then enter the going crowd because they all look full not awful so I rub the last fray of armour left tucked in the crook of my elbow skin and I fake being like them but I am not in the right place and the doorways are so far apart and dark beyond that baked pie feeling that never gets eaten just sits inside the oven and keeps being and smelling and tasting like it's meant to except that it's not doing its job properly and if anyone ever did want a bite they would be deep in the pastry before they knew the pie was empty

Mains at 23
when I meat him, something about white and horses and his full set of gently worn armour makes me bake the feeling that I am in need of something, something that maybe feels like food but is not food but is maybe him and he has never had this flavour pie before for his people prefer things that are liquid and proofed, not smoke or dense dough so he never had to go to the dairy on his own as a kid not until he owned his own life because that's how it happens for him and now he owns a car that can take him somewhere to be alone except he's not actually alone not like I do alone and he has no something smelling like something he should have but can't taste, like my crust crumbling at his lips.

Rātapu/Aso Sā

For Dr Moana Jackson

We hui on Sundays like this,
us sisters of the honey sweet vā
it's like church, but more chur.

Today we make service in the sun of K's porch—
no format, no rules, we're off the clock
hongi, take off our shoes and see what happens.

It's autumn so we start light, dance the day
into her mahi toi studio
trestle tables wobbling

like our bellies
as we sway and laugh,
we're all teeth and ocean hips.

K steeps rongoā,
pours it into thick potted cups
the steam to aid inhalation,

we exhale, karakia, tatalo.
She tells us that
at your nehu yesterday another group, like us

had gathered on the floor
of the wharemate at Matahiwi Marae—
seated around your tūpāpaku

someone said it looked like Moana had his
'harem' with him. 'Not a harem, a coven'
shot back one of the wāhine.

We smile at this story,
bow our heads to the steam
and ask each other how we would service

in death—what would you ask for?
K names wāhine
standing ground at Matahiwi

to speak on the paepae.
Marama, Emma, the other Moana (formerly) Jackson,
each took their turn,

voice to the descendent wish
of the fallen tōtara
kua hinga te tōtara i te wao nui a Tāne.

Maringi noa ngā roimata
maligi loimata
we see oceans as she speaks

of wāhine Tūhoe carrying
Moana-Nui-a-Kiwa
stilled in their hands.

NICHOLAS WRIGHT

A Jar

Stands perpendicular to anything, this fly
slowed by winter degrees into thought,
the hand-wringing abstractions of a mind;
must seem a chore now, this sawing through
the knowable distances between the large windows.
Sometimes still upon the glass, otherwise
davening forth and back above, behind the eyes
or, I imagine, silent in unobserved diligence,
saccading in some back room—a shadow
on the retina, an ambulant hole or black aperture.
It seems impossible now to conclude.

To find oneself in this hiatus, between an early end
and the surprised beginning of another season.
I circumscribed my window companion
with a jar and page on which it stood, a stickler
upon the rows, its ink-leg shadows.
I walked the fly out to gentle and compound again
and separated page from glass
but it stayed with me inside the jar,
settled, a blur of rust in the emptiness
independent of nothing. And that was it.

The Monarch Without

This clotting we think and call it season.
Let this be. But here are seed-blown gutters
yellowed furrows, and every seeming thing is
a mind under way to the world
underway to ... well. Such is the matter at hand.
One new thing after another,
colour in drains dammed with succession,
chambered instars all itching to moult or
under-wise, thicken, carve arteries, wait
in veins, venules, capillaries. And here
you are: modern and ill-humoured, a head
full of heredity, sovereign of snot,
colour and sputum, clammy on a hill
at noon and no way to tell from ideal
the thing, nor thought from beloved pattern.
Ahead of the coming storm a fistful
of black stars are thrown across the grey mass,
a mind rearing tall in the great without,
and it comes to you to call them starlings
that raced ahead in the interstitium,
and at your feet to call these samaras,
papery vulvae showered all over,
the pavement splitting in ruts, gathering
about the roots of trees; finally,
here: the headless monarch for whom you bent
unfolded upon the lines of your palm
the slow beat of spotless hind wings, the black
thickness of veins, this intimate tunic
fit to sex, and confer identity.

MARIA McMILLAN

Sixteen Ways to Incite a Revolution

1.
You ask your mother to start one for you. She says, I tried, I tried. How do you think I met your father? But it didn't work and now I'm tired. And you say, well, you need to try harder. And your mother says, no one wants my kind of revolution. And your little sister says, perhaps, Maggie, you should start your own revolution. You say, I'm just a child, I should not have to shoulder that responsibility. Really, *how* do you incite a revolution? Your mother says, well, you need a cause. What cause do you want? And you say, any of them. You say, all of them.

2.
Through a series of dangerous and illicit experiments you discover that your cat loves to eat plastic and his powerful digestive juices transform it into rich sweet-smelling compost. You mount an expedition into the nearby parklands where your cat comes from, and collect all the wild kittens you can find. There are 37 of them and they all eat plastic. You make them a ladder between the ceiling cavity (where they live and where you toss your recycling, and the sound of them crunching brittle plastic is as comforting as rain on a tin roof) and the garden (where they dig and crouch and fertilise the soil). You and the cats are content. You grow giant pineapples and plums and the house is very warm. The cats begin to breed and you give away the kittens, and the kittens grow up and have kittens which grow up and have kittens. The Great Age of the Cat is upon us. There are house cats and dump cats, and coastal cats that peer over the sides of jetties and use their paws to bat at the plastic that floats by, which they delicately pick up and put in their mouths. The land is a mass of moving fur. The oceans are abundant once more. The cats all look like Tuesday.

3.
Under your bed you find an old square envelope full of seeds. On the envelope, in what appears hastily scrawled writing, it says *Revolution (nice). Sow directly where plants are to grow. Will spread, 2004.* It's before you were even born but you are, by nature, optimistic.

4.
You breathe in and out. In, out. In, out. The trees around your house breathe with you. You know they are connected by a vast underground fungal network through which they transmit complex messages to each other. You look deep into yourself, and know that you too are a tree and your mother is a tree and your father and your sister. And all your friends and their friends. And you are also fungi. And also you are the birds in the tree making incessant chirps. And you know then, perhaps you always knew it, that you need never talk again. It is superfluous. We are all connected in deep mysterious ways. You stare into mid-distance pondering. You let all your worries float away and for about 45 years or 45 minutes—what indeed is time?—you send healing thoughts to all humanity and your sister says, the thing about the best episode of *Doctor Who* is ... Maggie, what happened to you? Your eyes have gone very weird, no offence.

5.
You google revolution. You have ready a notebook and a sharpened pencil. The first result is *Makeup revolution*. The next result is *Revolution Beauty*. The third result is *It's time for your beauty makeup revolution: Official stockist*. You turn your device off. You find all the devices in the house, and all the devices in the neighbours' houses. You collect them into a pile and you use a bone-handled knife to prise open the plastic casing. You remove all the motherboards. With tweezers and a torch and a magnifying glass you remove the precious metals from the motherboards. And then you smash the motherboards and the casings and the screens into the smallest, most irreparable smithereens. And then you fashion the precious metals into a ring with words that circle it: *but the revolution is not made up.*

6.
You decide you will eat no hedgehog flesh ever again. You start the hashtag #hedgehogsarenotforeating and #thenohedgehogfleshproject. You do a daily video updating your followers on how it is to not eat hedgehog, and how you've changed as a person since your commitment to a hedgehog-flesh-free life. How calm and terrific it is not eating hedgehogs and how luminous your skin is now. You write a book *My Year Without Eating Hedgehogs* and you curate a collection of amusing anecdotes about non-hedgehog eaters through history. You are humbled. You do your best to honour those who have gone before. You release a range of fast-food products that use no hedgehog products, using a smiling hedgehog as your logo. It is quickly followed by a book of hedgehog-free recipes. A woman you have never met claims your logo uses their uncredited artwork. They show a hand-drawn picture of a smiling hedgehog that looks nothing like yours. It's not even cute. They use the hashtag #anotherrippedoffartist. They start the hashtag #thenonohedgehogfleshprojectproject. You trend on Twitter. You invite #anotherrippedoffartist for a conversation and a hot chocolate. The chocolate is sweet and hot. The woman weeps in your arms. She admits to drawing the hedgehog after seeing your logo. She was so lonely, she only wanted sympathy, she only wanted friends. You are sad for her but suddenly terribly bored by it all. You gift your company to #anotherrippedoffartist. She is full of ideas. She starts an immediate plan to pull #thenohedgehogfleshproject back from the brink of cancellation. She will run a new refreshed social media campaign that features a series of abject and humiliating apologies. She is radiantly happy. After she leaves you find a book you thought you'd lost and an interesting new hollow in your bed. The cat jumps on you.

7.
You do your own research. You write a list of all the features of all the best revolutions there have ever been. There are 17 commonly occurring features but no revolution has had all 17 features. With an 0.4 Artline 200 you draw a Venn diagram with 17 intersecting labelled circles. In the middle of the diagram, in the middle of the page, there it is.

8.
One night you lay a bear trap in the garden. In the morning you find a very small, and quite angry actually, revolution in the trap. It has the most beautiful long silky feet.

9.
You know your own mind, which is as free and strong as a goose. You decide one afternoon to fly the Revolutionary Flag of Immutable Tolerance out your window. The night is long, the wind is a bit sad, and the flag is a dark patch in darkness but you are not a bit afraid. In the morning you stay in bed feeling awkward. In the afternoon you look out the window and all the neighbours have the Revolutionary Flag of Immutable Tolerance flying out their windows. You are immensely cheered and you call out from your window, three cheers for the revolution, and they call back hip hip hooray, hip hip hooray, hip hip hooray. Everyone then runs from their houses to the street and dances and drinks lemonade and hands out flowers to passers-by and you are so happy that it has all begun and tastes so nice. And then an Old Somebody says, yes, yes! We will encourage our neighbours to fly the Revolutionary Flag of Immutable Tolerance out their windows, and the crowd roars, Yes, yes! And yes, says the Old Somebody, they will encourage their neighbours, and then our village will encourage the towns, and then we will be able to see anyone who is not flying a Revolutionary Flag of Immutable Tolerance. Isn't it wonderful? Don't you see? We will see who they are, those terrible turnips who are not Immutably Tolerant, and we can look up their names and tell each other and they will be banished forever. Yes, yes? Oh he is gleeful. Oh he is pleased with himself. And the crowd roars, Yes yes! No, no! and begins to laugh. The Old Somebody, who himself was banished unfairly for many years, looks so sad and so angry that you think the sky will crack. You think everything will run backwards and it will all be lost. But then the Old Somebody joins in the laughter and laughs the hardest of anyone, so the lemonade in the glass he is holding swells like an ocean and the floating mint leaves dance the gay fandango.

10.

You become very good at harmonica. You band together with all the harmonica players in the country and march to Parliament demanding justice. Your demands are not met. You stand on the steps of Parliament playing harmonica. Still your demands are not met. You set up tents on the Parliament lawns, and you work in shifts, playing glorious harmonica all day and all through the starry night.

11.

There is a place you can write to. They've been keeping the same revolution alive since Paris in 1968. If you ask, they'll send you some. So you get some old revolution sent to you and there are very long instructions about how to keep it alive. The instructions are photocopied, and the ink is very dark in places, and the copy they sent you is not new but so well used the folds have gone as soft as linen. The instructions tell you how often you must feed the revolution and the best flour to use, how to pour off the hooch, and how you must not let it grow too fast or it will die, and how you can store it in the refrigerator and not feed it for a week or so if you're going away or a bit weary. Your revolution begins to grow. Sometimes you take a piece and shape it into a loaf and bake it. Sometimes you put some in a jar and leave it on the doorstep of a neighbour who has asked for it.

12.

It is harder and harder to find shops that stock needles, and a clean needle with no splits is terribly important. You must attach the needle piece carefully to the arm—nothing must touch the threads of the needle. You turn the switch on, then the machine on, and then the record will begin to turn. You lift the arm into a position exactly between the smooth edge of the record and the grooves where the music is crouching, mouth open, waiting to sing. Then you use the switch to lower the arm. You may need to balance a coin on the arm to keep it steady. In the 1950s there were four possible speeds that records could be played at. The rare $16\frac{2}{3}$ revolutions per minute, $33\frac{1}{3}$ rpm, 45 rpm and, most revolutionary of all, 78 revolutions per minute.

13.
One day in spring you find a nest of tiny revolutions in your garden. They must have fallen from a tree. You look around for their mother but she is nowhere to be seen. They are so small, their feathers have not even grown yet. You know what you must do. The whole bit. The eyedropper and the sweetened water, the insides of their mouths the most brilliant red.

14.
Someone is chopping down a forest so you move permanently to the top of a tree and the machines can't do anything. Other people climb trees near yours and move in. You whistle to each other in a secret code. You build rope-walks between the treetops. The people living in houses nearby bring you hot soup the colour of road cones. The tractors begin to rust.

15.
You paint the most beautiful picture in the world. Certain brushstrokes capture the tragedy of existence, others the exquisite uncertainty of it all, still others tremulous joy, and others again the unspoken hopes of old dogs. Your painting is so tall and so wide that, in order to look at it, people must crowd into the cabin of a crane. The crane moves slowly across the entire surface of the painting. Poets write about the painting, a new ballet is choreographed, a fictionalised account of your life is turned into a musical. People leave the gallery having seen your painting and they are exquisitely quiet, or they look puzzled and say, I don't know but there's something about that painting, or they talk excitedly to each other, using wild hand gestures and rubbing their hair in exultation exclaiming, we must make the world worthy of that wondrous work.

16.
First you get your revolution. Then you eat it.

LIZ BRESLIN

ACC Lullaby

on a scale of one to one how do you feel
about intimacy on a scale of starting in five
four three how hard do you find
it to look away look now away on a scale
of one to ten can you cry without screens
if five is never and ten is always and one is i
have no problem with this on a scale
of sliding how do you brake on a break
from the scales on a scale of voices do yours
have needs on a scale of a mermaid can you
catch the tide if household tasks had scales
do you see straight lines when you close
your eyes on a scale of nine to five how
many days have you missed on a scale
of maths to glitter to the incubus
on a scale of how do you sleep on a scale
of one to ten nine eight six five if you think
for a moment now about sex if you how
many last days would you on a scale of why
if you think now for a moment about your
commitments intimates intrusive ties
think think think think think think think
your body wash you do you do you
on a scale of improvement does your dignity
on a scale of invested how have you not
if you wash over the scales over your whole
your whole on a scale of hungry how can
you eat if ten is always and five is never and
one is one and i have no problem with this

MEDB CHARLETON

Letter to the Editor

I wrote a poem with a peacock in it
and then I read Stevens' poem with the peacocks
and the leaves and the commensurability
and similitude of all things
and then someone said,
'Do you write poems with conversations in them?'
And I said, 'Do you have conversations with poems in them?'
And then I wrote a poem with a conversation in it
but I'm still thinking about peacocks,
in autumn, leaves or feathers
burnished by light, and commonality.

In Search Of

Isolation; islanded in a concrete sea. Summer moving across the caged skywalk. I'm looking for words like beacons in this nightmarish world. True to form the picture changes and there I am as a child before the Garden of Earthly Delights where people air-kiss and the poems keep coming and I hear God talking to me although I can't be sure saying don't you know other people's dreams are dull as trout's eyes when the gleam has gone and the river tremors its last through it?

RUBEN MITA

No Good

See the way she turns and sends it straight?
That's the way a fencepost sings in hail.
That's the way the wind strums the guitar in the night.
That's the way we sit up, afraid.

See the way the birds advance
and the bees hesitate?
The tūī cut Thursday from Friday.
That's the way an engine coughs in clean country air.
That's the way a bank teller wakes from the best dream.

It's not quite inspiration,
something more like
throwing darts, left-handed, blindfolded,
into a laptop screen
(see the way my arm straightens though).

That's the way words land.
That's the way phone alarms reveal
two lambs in the botanic gardens,
two birds singing from the headstone.

It's not quite a confession,
something more like
the way a cake lies in a cool evening,
when there's light on the deck,
and someone richer two doors down
has the fire going.
That's the way things watch and wait.

That's the way a minute hand dreams of thirteen.

And the two birds sing:
'No good,
 no good,
 no good.'

LISA ONLAND

Stare Down the Sea

Erin noticed the leak on Sunday night, after switching on the dishwasher and locking the back door. It made a copper-orange circle on the ceiling in front of her wardrobe. From the centre a large drop of water formed and fell, joining the puddle on the floor.

She worried about the cost before contemplating the cause, still waiting on a response from the personnel agency. 'Things are tough,' the recruiter had said, slipping her resumé back into his folder. 'We've got nineteen other applicants for this role alone.' The position involved working reception at a twenty-four-hour gym. Erin didn't know which was more grim: that nineteen other people were after the job or that she probably wouldn't get it.

She wondered if there was a pool of water forming above the ceiling plaster. How much water before it cracked and gave way? She had never been in the attic. Wasn't sure how everything up there worked. It was supposed to keep the rain out, and yet. She looked down at the puddle on the floor.

The house sat inside a tsunami evacuation zone. A blue sign at the end of the street depicted a stick figure fleeing a trio of deadly white waves. Fated to meet swirling destruction in the wake of a bad quake. They're saying it's not far away—the quake to end all quakes. Erin once dated a guy who used to work for the Earthquake Commission. He told her the safest place to live in Wellington was further north, up past the gorge. Better to have rock under the foundation, less chance of the ground swallowing her house. Technically, her mother's house. She was in a care home now, early-onset Alzheimer's. Once her father's life insurance payment ran out, the family would sell. Until then, Erin lived there for free. Christine, two years older and more mother than sister, hated her for it.

'What do you know about fixing a leaky roof?' Erin asked Marcus the following evening. She had gone around to his place when he got home from school. Teaching not studying. Mostly year 10. She'd known right away he had a tolerance for bullshit.

Marcus picked up his vape from the side table and lay back in bed.

'Tile or steel?'

'Steel.'

He took a drag and shook his head. 'No idea.'

Marcus had a flatmate, Simon. He was a teacher too. Once she'd walked in on him at the kitchen table, making his way through a packet of chocolate digestives. He stood and put them away when she appeared, as though she had interrupted a hallowed ritual.

'Is your roof leaking?' Marcus asked, rolling to one side so he could look at her.

She nodded.

'That sucks.'

Erin nodded again. She liked Marcus. She liked that he took his time. Made sure she finished first.

When he got up to use the toilet, she pulled the dented bottle opener from the pocket of her discarded jeans and slid it back in the dresser drawer. She took the decorative pen down from the windowsill, turning it over in her hands. There was an inscription engraved along one side. *21! Love Mum & Ian.* She dropped it in her purse. Erin liked to carry something of his with her, back home, to work, when she visited her mother. Together they'd never ventured beyond his flat but this way they didn't have to.

If it wasn't an earthquake or a tsunami (or both), then it would be the rain that did them in. Flooding the city, slips closing the roads. The hundred-year flood now an annual occurrence. Wettest winter on record, that's what they were saying. Across the ditch it was the fires. A morbid game of Would You Rather: death by drowning or immolation? No contest, she'd choose to burn. More painful, yes, but less time for contemplation.

When she was ten and her father still alive, they'd gone to the local school during a tsunami evacuation. With over a hundred people crammed into the assembly hall, there had been a long line for the toilets. She remembered looking down at her pink leggings as they darkened. After that, she insisted on staying home, preferring to die in a roil of sea foam than face public humiliation.

While she waited to hear back from the recruiter, Erin cleaned people's houses. She was paid by a company in Auckland that scheduled appointments through an elaborate online booking system. She had seen the ads pop up on her own feed. Apparently she also fit their target demographic. The company liked to promise things they couldn't deliver. Like a full house clean in two hours. They gave her a checklist and she always finished late. She didn't get paid for anything over the two-hour time slot, and clients complained if something on the list wasn't done. As she finished each room she took a photo. She submitted the photos to the company at the end of the job, along with a status report. She didn't get paid for that either. But she had gone into debt for a business degree—the least she could do was make use of her university-grade admin skills.

Though not a fan of the cleaning, she did enjoy looking through her clients' homes. She didn't take stuff like she did with Marcus but she made a mental note of the things she would. A 3B1 notebook with the word LYRIX written across the front in black Vivid. A yellow plastic comb she found under a bathroom vanity, a single grey hair trapped in its teeth.

The leak was getting worse. The copper stain had spread, mottling the paint around it like a virus. Inside the wardrobe a black shadow of mould crept along the ceiling. Her clothes hung limply from the rail below.

'Call a roofing company,' her sister admonished her over the phone. 'I'm not your landlord. If you're living there rent free, you can pay for basic repairs.'

The first company Erin called said she'd need to pay a $300 deposit. She told them she'd call them back. She opened her banking app and checked her balance, then pulled her sheets and pillow off the bed and moved into her mother's old room.

'Wouldn't it be crazy if I booked a cleaning and you showed up?' Marcus said, shoving a handful of fries into his mouth.

Growing up, Erin's mother likened eating in bed to a hate crime. Marcus's mum must have had a different opinion. She sat cross-legged on his bed and picked at her Filet-o-Fish even though she was starving. It was only a couple of blocks away but he'd insisted on Uber Eats. They spent so much time in here she could conjure every detail of his bedroom with her eyes closed.

'I'll clean your place for free if you want,' she said.

Marcus stopped eating, gave her a funny smile. 'Ha, I'm not after a clean. I was just thinking it would be one of those odd coincidences, you know? Like seeing your boss at the supermarket.'

She tried to visit their mother every Saturday. Without ever discussing it, Christine went on a different day. It was for the best, really. The three of them didn't get on well enough to be in a room together. Erin didn't mind the visits. Their mother was oddly tranquil in her poky little room. TV on, crochet blanket around her shoulders.

'Did your father drop you off?' she asked.

Erin nodded. Christine had told her not to lie. She should treat their mother as she would anyone else, not someone whose mind was unravelling like an old jumper.

'Has he gone home? Why didn't he come in?' her mother implored, eyes welling.

'There's ice-cream in the boot. He doesn't want it to melt.'

Lying was more humane.

The lines smoothed on her mother's face. 'Of course.'

'What are you watching?' Erin looked at the small screen suspended from the wall. It was some kind of children's show. Puppets and primary colours.

'*The Love Boat*,' her mother replied.

Erin unpacked the biscuits she had smuggled past the nurse and squeezed next to her mother in bed. They watched *The Love Boat*, getting crumbs in the sheets.

Erin slipped up only once. She knew before she took it that it would be missed, but the heart-shaped pendant had called to her. Practically put itself in her pocket. The client complained. She received a polite email from the company in Auckland saying they no longer required her services. She didn't know many other people keen to provide that kind of service for what they were paying. She had already tried to skip dusting the skirting boards and still couldn't get through the list in the allotted time.

'Do you want to void the insurance?' Her sister called on the bus ride home. Erin sat at the back, a bag of groceries at her feet.

'I stopped by today to check Mum's mail and saw the bucket in your bedroom. Did you call a roofer?' In the background Erin could hear her nephew crying. She wondered why Christine had gone into her room.

'I did,' she said. Not a lie. 'They're booked up for months.' A lie.

'Then call someone else! Jesus, Erin. It will only get worse the more you ignore it.'

'I know,' she lied again.

The rain hadn't stopped for days. The city was melting around her, awash in grey mush. She considered calling someone else about the roof. But no matter who she called, the amount in her bank account wasn't getting any bigger.

The recruiter left a voicemail. She hadn't made the cut. 'Best of luck,' the man said knowingly as he hung up, sure she would need it.

Erin thought about a time when things in her life looked very different. Promising, even. As though she had been walking a wire and only realised when her foot slipped.

'I know about you taking stuff and putting it back.'

She got up then, pulled on her pants.

'Hang on,' Marcus said, reaching for her arm, fingers brushing her wrist. 'I'm not mad.'

She moved away, shrugging on her shirt. She spotted her bra on the floor and bent to pick it up, shoving it in her back pocket.

'Erin,' he called from the bed as she grabbed her bag. 'Erin!' he called again as she stepped into her boots and closed the bedroom door behind her.

When the quake came, Erin was in the bath. The water rippled. She rested her palm on the surface, feeling the shudder with her fingertips. There was a crash from the kitchen. Her towel swayed on the shower rail above. She counted silently in her head. *Long or strong be gone.* After getting dressed, she made herself some toast and turned on the TV. 7.1. Off the coast. Civil Defence had issued a tsunami warning. She finished her toast and turned off the TV. She went to her bedroom and looked at the bucket, the steady drip from the ceiling. Then she opened the wardrobe and pulled out her backpack. Erin had no intention of joining her neighbours in the assembly hall at the local school. She set off in search of higher ground.

When she knocked, it was Simon who answered.
'Is Marcus home?'
He paused, considering. Marcus appeared in the hallway behind him.
'Come in,' he said, reaching for her hand and leading her past his flatmate into the house.
He closed the door to his bedroom and she put her backpack down on the floor. Then picked it up again, not wanting to be presumptuous.
'There's a tsunami warning,' she said.
He nodded. 'Do you want to stay here?'
Erin shrugged.
'You can if you want,' he said.
'What do *you* want?'
'For you to stay. And to stop nicking my stuff.'
'I got fired from that cleaning job.'
'How come?'
'Stealing.'
Marcus laughed. She smiled.
'You hungry?'

Her phone rang at the Indian restaurant. Marcus was spooning chicken saagwala onto his plate. It was her sister. Erin thought about the house, the leak. Maybe it would all wash away.
'Are you still at home?' Christine asked. 'Do you need somewhere to go?'
Erin heard the concern in her voice. It sounded strange. Nice though.
'I'm all right,' she said.
There was silence on the other end.
'Do you remember that time when we were kids?' her sister asked.
'And we were stuck in the school hall?'
'And you pissed yourself?'
She was laughing now, or maybe crying, tears running down her cheeks.

TIM GRGEC

Swimming to Australia

I was sure Mum said she was only swimming out to that rock.
I was sure that's what she said, but she also grinned
and said something about swimming all the way to Australia.

I know she's a good swimmer, but even for her
that would be far, I think, all the way to Australia.
She disappears under every wave,

past her waist—past where Petar and I are allowed up to.
Petar is building a castle
and Dad is still reading in his chair

while her splashing limbs get smaller
and smaller in the distance,
and I think maybe she really is going that far, swimming to another country.

The sunscreen on my hands flavours my chips
and I have to look away for a moment,
before staring back at what I think is Mum

out there somewhere, her floating head
just above the water. I stare for a while longer
before I realise I've lost her

and that what I thought was her head was just one of those buoy things
bobbling for faraway boats and ships.
Then I see she's actually a piece of driftwood.

No, a shark fin, circling backwards and forwards,
which doesn't explain where Mum's got to.
The tide bites our towels,

so Dad gets us to pack up our buckets
and carry our boogie boards back to the car,
even though she's still out there,

and I think what if it really is a shark that's replaced her?
Or worse, if no one seems to notice
as it slowly makes its way to shore,

wraps itself in her towel
and comes home with us
in the front seat next to Dad.

I never really wanted a shark for a mother
as I look out again at the dot on the horizon,
small enough to hold in my fingers.

Midnight Tea

She examines the face I've grown into—
my father's nose, she says, her smile,
trying to find the words
after all these years.

We have a lot to cover, my mother and I,
awake to the quiet complaints of the house.
Once familiar to me was the hum of the dishwasher
gurgling through its cycle, the cicadas,

my bedsheet damp from sweat.
We share tea in the kitchen, worried about each other
it seems—she about my sleepless
red eyes,

me, something about her no longer being around.
She can't believe how tall I am now—
an inheritance from her father,
of course, and the fathers before him—

as I try to hurry her through
smartphones and ebooks
and all the things that weren't around
when she was,

which is important for her to make sense of
but somehow beside the point
when there's still
so much more to say.

I try to show her the poems I've written
since then, books and articles published,
the two master's degrees framed in the hallway
which, having been fixed

in the same place for years, are misplaced
at the very moment I need them.
All the words I've ever written
spill out of their margins

to take on lives
and arrangements of their own,
unrecognisable to me or her in the darkness.
This can be easily explained, I say,

and *I haven't even got to Issey,
our plans for marriage and children,*
now fumbling my lines,
unsure what exactly

I'm supposed to be telling my mother,
as she rinses our cups
and excuses herself once again
out the unlocked front door.

ANNABELLE O'MEARA

The Garden Tour

Carol felt diminished. She'd foolishly agreed to sit back seat middle when they picked up Fiona in Khandallah. Now her left foot was stuck under Fiona's tote bag, her bunion hurt and they were only at Upper Hutt. From the front passenger seat, Jude tried conducting the meeting they were meant to have during the week but no one could make it. She held up the garden tour brochure and called for bids on where to start but the nausea-threatening bends on the Remutaka Hill road cast a grim, silent pall over them. Carol noticed Sally, white-faced and silent behind the wheel, was paying far too much attention to the EV power gauge and very little to the precipitous road. Hope that prosecco's all right in the boot, she said. Still no one spoke. At Featherston, conversation resumed and they decided to sort the itinerary in Greytown over coffee but everywhere was full and noisy. They returned to the car cradling takeaway cups, meeting reconvened, route agreed and Fiona was nominated navigator—Sally had said no to the sat nav as any more dashboard data would simply exhaust her. Trish would be the narrator, announcing each garden with a brief synopsis from the brochure. Trish worked in marketing.

By lunchtime they'd done three gardens and looked forward to an afternoon of peonies, lavender and old homesteads. Carol, now in jandals, hinted at popping back to Greytown so she could buy a sunhat. She said the forecast had been wrong. Loud eyeroll. They headed east as the sun beat down and the Wairarapa heat called for full air con, again vetoed by Sally, citing unnecessary use of the EV's power. Windows were lowered, hairstyles took off. At Brancepeth homestead, Carol suggested the tepid prosecco should be consumed before it boiled and exploded in the boot. She'd brought paper cups, she said. An hour passed under the generous shade of an English oak, the mood lightened, shoes were kicked off and complexions crimsoned. It was all lovely, they agreed.

Later at the Air BnB, more bubbles came out while Jude plated the cheese and dips, loudly announcing the provenance and price of each cheese, but everyone swooped without homage nor compliment. She made a mental note to do Edam and a cheap brie next time. Room allocations had been decided by the toss of a dice found among the host's board games. By the second bottle, reflections of the day's gardens became harsher, bolder, and details of statuary, shaded glades and herbaceous borders were torn apart like shredded lettuce. Later, at the restaurant, a prandial calmness settled them after the main course and a more charitable discourse ensued. The day had been fabulous and the gardens on the whole were lovely. Can't wait for day two, they said. Back at the house, Sally said she'd recharge overnight and went out to look for the car.

    By four o'clock on Sunday they were back on the hill road to Wellington and Carol sat in the front. Tired, toured out and a little hungover, they swapped best-moment stories and favourite new plants, and mused on their own green-thumb aspirations. Trish thought she'd go in for damasks next year, and Jude, whom they'd all considered a tad staid, said she'd totally fallen for Pierre de Ronsard. Fiona murmured that she adored everything and felt like rusticating. They all stared out the window till someone said let's do Kāpiti next year. Sally wished they'd all just shut up. She was at ten percent and they were only at Petone. By way of distraction, she announced she intended speaking to Ian about buying a weekender in Martinborough. Loud eyeroll.

TIM UPPERTON

Caselberg House, Broad Bay

Nothing I have ever written, or might still write, has
been worth half the anguish that my life has been to me.
                              —Charles Brasch

This tranquil place, I almost hate it
the way I almost hate poetry.
The sky, the sea—what is there to say?
Still, I try to say it. The sky, the sea,
rinsed and empty like a wineglass.
A cat, rather fat and contented-looking,
has ambled through the open door.
He pushes hard against my hand,
and I don't think I need to tell you
he is my best friend in the world.
All I want to do these long afternoons
is stroke this cat's rough fur,
feel his electricity at my fingertips.
Hello, I say, and he doesn't answer,
he's a cat—but who ever answers,
really? Who is your friend,
who can be your friend in this world?
Caught in the prickly foliage of a tōtara,
high up, a red balloon! Remember how,
at the end of a birthday party,
the parents would give you a balloon
to take home? A little air, a little colour.
The sea this evening, through the window,
is like ruffled silk. Creatures move
beneath its surface that I will never know.
Hello. I'm glad you're here.

MARK EDGECOMBE

Heaven's Suburbs

Heaven's suburbs are found where railway lines
end, are mapped over doorwells in trains that send

their cargo of pilgrims in both directions,
bask in names like Bethel Heights, Apocalypse Park.

From them, if you squint hard enough,
you will sometimes fancy you make out Heaven itself,

or when crossing the tracks, pausing between the rails
to stare up the line beyond where they veer, you might

surmise Heaven's shimmer in waves rising
from steel. People in Heaven seldom have reason

to visit its suburbs, but suburbanites like,
as often as they can, to make the trip to Heaven's

Square. They like the trees and river there,
the Statue of the Fallen Angel, the replica Tower

of Babel, its permanent scaffold and proprietary
nod to all the tongues that are native there.

They like the food stalls, the falafel, the lamb,
the buskers and bookstores and spires and throne,

the billboards climbing buildings, their polyglot boasts:
CIUDAD DE DIOS ... GOTTES EIGENE STADT ...

They like the way the words of God turn buildings'
corners in pixelated letters, the patois, the argots,

the rhyming slangs, the free newspapers and swank
magazines, and most heavenly of all—waiters,

unbidden, proffering dessert menus at each meal's end.
On such celestial nights, when the sun seems loath to set,

they linger as long as they can, catch at last the last train
back, stop on the tipsy staggerwalk home

for cash for the sitter, the one who's using the wifi
to watch Netflix on her phone, who has eaten the plums

she was asked not to touch, and whose boyfriend, bare-
arsed, hides in the garden, heart all aflutter,

a kawakawa leaf concealing his crotch.

ZOË MEAGER

We didn't notice when the trees along the boundary line went missing

They were *ponderosa* or *radiata* or something. A windbreak planted before our time, by the same bloke perhaps who took an axe to the old farm and sold it off in odd-shaped blocks. We did talk about how great some of those sunsets were lately—just not the mechanics of it, how those missing trees left so much more of the sky on show. We honestly didn't notice either when we lost half an acre off the far end of the property; the school holidays had just started, and Sophie got her first period, and then a couple of the hens got egg-bound. We did catch on when half the potting shed disappeared though—where were our gloves and trowels, the lettuce seedlings and the extra plastic pots? After that, the dogs were taken (by who, and where?). We nursed beers on the porch and bent our necks to our phones but we couldn't find anything to explain why things weren't there any more. Later, when the kids came home from the neighbours', instead of scooting out back to kick a ball around, they clattered around in the house, which then fell silent. That was lovely for a while, to be fair. We ended up stuffing around with the ball ourselves, until it went off somewhere between the ferns and blousy hydrangeas down the side of the house. (And there was another thing we didn't notice: no more prickles in the lawn, and no more bees.) It was the light that was snatched away next. Daylight and starlight and moonlight all failed, so we groped our way into the cave of our house and found all the house lights and lamps and flashlights mute to the touch. We tried lighting a candle but the flame shied away from the wick. We called for Alex and Sophie as we bumped through the shifting rooms of our house, but our children were not there and we were not able to find them. Eventually things all folded in on themselves. We lost the sound of our own voices and when we reached out to hold hands, couldn't feel them. We woke sometimes in the night, or stumbled through what we thought was day, and felt around for things that just weren't there any more, and we tried to imagine everything as it had been before, but even our imaginations were lost. We couldn't remember: a broom shushing over wet concrete, the squish and hook of the cat's paw, or the shape of those trees along the boundary line, turning charcoal as the sun fell down, like all the Christmases we had ever known set out in one neat row and burning.

BRETT CROSS

the indefinite article

the indefinite article
the noun

considering
the noun

a dog wags
park green

trees
dark fir

flip
back

through
oneself

the hula hoop
spins

dusk
drops

gloom
all is gloom

the frisbee
catches the fading

light
the kids

are unconfused
the park is a park

for the length
there is length

then the shadows
pass

the park
in the suburbs

the bark
of the dog

the indefinite
articles

EMMA NEALE

The Moth-eyed Steeplechase Horse

At a farmstay in Routeburn
we offer small coins of carrot
to a thoroughbred who lips them up:
our hands held flat as picnic plates
over her paddock fence.

We wait, as if in her amber eyes
we'll find each horse-thought formed
as clear as honeyed cells of wax.

Globed, deep presence,
she takes us in
and we are dreams that flow
easily as bleached driftwood
down a slow river current.

Time piles in cloud towers
as magpie song spirals;
we look away, catch small hot dots
of white, pink, gold,
as the sun glints deep in the grass
like dropped wedding rings.

I look back, to see the horse
has one dark pupil shaped like a moth,
its scallop-edged wings spreadeagled.
Look at your eye! I want to say,
as if she wears a rare jewel;
yet as our stare expands she seems to see

into each and every human weakness.
I am as thrown as I was, long years ago:

a sadhu, his ochre robes in ropes of rags,
hair twisted in tree bark strips,
wooden staff in his slim grip,
stoic, singular and alone,
locked his eyes with mine
as I stood there with my palm
clasped inside my husband's
and I felt a catapult of fear:
this man's receptiveness to pain and drift
against my clinging to love
like a moth's egg to a leaf tip
exposed all that was wrong
and false in us: yes, even the way

I want to hold this morning
under an agapanthus sky
with a gentle, moth-eyed horse
as if the thread of language
could ever weave a hide
against the hook and sting of loss
when we carry it
deep as the mare does
the sprint, the vault,
in her hocks, her fetlocks.

JAMES PASLEY

A Name to Remember

Dean liked to think he hadn't had to work for it, but everyone knows how hungry he'd been, how he'd bugged Barry, the editor, until he was hired as a sub, and how, once he was in, he made himself indispensable. He made it seem like he had been there his whole life. And it worked—in a few short years he worked his way up to become one of the country's top crime reporters. At twenty-six, he was covering major court cases, following them through to the grisly, hollow, knee-weakening end. He took his stories further than anyone else. He was respected. It was all up, until it wasn't.

Now, he is a solid man in his mid-thirties. His dark hair is thinning. Everyone knows something is wrong. Not that he's over the hill. Far from it. He still possesses that hint of something darker all good crime reporters have—he is hardened, happy to get his hands dirty, has the requisite cold lizard look that makes a lifestyle journalist wilt. He is first rate. His is a byline to read. But on Monday, after a year of long nights arguing with his fiancée about counselling, money, holidays and the concept of mutual respect, he will hand in his resignation. He has accepted a government job. They are moving to Wellington.

He hates himself already. The problem is he knows what happens if he stays. He will get promoted, first to editor, later to management, and in a few years' time he will find himself afloat; his foot will have slipped from the pedal. He will be unhappy, stalking about the newsroom, dead faced, laconic, bordering on sullen. Decorated and respected, he will be tied to a desk when he should be out there, on the road, chasing ambulances.

So it's decided and tonight he is going bowling with the team one last time. It's late December and this is the closest thing they will get to a Christmas party. Barry had another dinner, so Dean, as the most senior reporter, is in charge.

He looks back at them now, his puffing and pale peers, their T-shirts sticking to sweaty backs, lanyards dangling from curved necks, and thinks despondently about their lack of self-care. Then he softens. It's been a long year and they're exhausted. The lifts didn't work so they had to climb six flights of stairs to get here. And worst of all, they don't actually want to be here. They're ready to go, ready to drive back to their small home towns, to eat a good meal and answer the questions that come tied to it. They will, just like he used to, tell their families about Auckland, the big city, about the newspaper, about the life they lead. They will make it sound glamorous, forgetting to mention click quotas and the slow days spent scrolling through Facebook looking for a quick hit piece.

'No shoes, right?' the bowling manager says.

'Do we want shoes?' Dean asks. Then, without waiting for an answer, he confirms they will take shoes. In the silence that follows, he clears his throat and tells the manager they need eight pairs.

He doesn't tell the manager that two of his reporters will get their size wrong and be back in a few minutes to swap them. But late on Monday afternoon, after formally resigning, he will tell Barry. He will ask, how can they be trusted to cover courts or elections when they can't recall their own shoe size? And afterwards, in the cold, dusky silence, he will laugh.

After everyone's paid for themselves, Dean buys a beer. He tells Owen, who is always nearby, that he would buy a round but company policy forbids it.

He's not lying. The policy exists. There have been too many incidents: the sub-editor exposing himself to the intern, the US correspondent with the wandering hands, the photographer who got 'lost' in the women's bathroom. It is always men.

'No worries,' Owen says.

Dean feels bad now as he slides the three-toned shoes on. He dislikes having to make the reporters pay for their own bowling. He dislikes knowing how much, how little, each of them earns. He dislikes the way once the shoes are on everything becomes loose and slippery.

He looks around. For a year or so, back when he was at university, he spent every weekend here. He hung out with a regular group he has since lost touch with. For a while it was a second home. Nothing has changed. The dank odour remains; it's the same dark cavernous hall with a few sparse bulbs blinking sadly over the lanes; the arcade remains empty, its main drawcard, the basketball hoop, is wrenched to the side meaning it's impossible to make a swish. The kitchen, with its proud D for cleanliness, remains closed.

The party splits into two. Four to each lane. Dean ends up with Owen, Sophie and Tessa. They begin to bowl. Sophie and Tessa don't care—they are busy discussing holiday plans—but Dean and Owen care. Dean is flushed. He wants to win.

Owen wants to win too, perhaps even more. For the past ten days he has got to work early, pitched dozens of story ideas, been told to proceed with none of them. Barry has done most of the head shaking, but on the mornings he's been late or otherwise engaged, Dean has happily said no. Owen makes his calls from a private booth so no one can hear. He is shy. He is nervous. Every time he gets something wrong—bothers the wrong person, exaggerates a quote, misrepresents the readership of their paper—he rolls his chair over to Dean's desk and asks if it's serious enough to warrant having to tell Barry.

So far, Dean has told him not to worry.

Dean bowls a couple of times but fails to find his form. He can't get low enough. He buys another beer. When he sits back down he looks at the score. Owen is pulling ahead.

He drinks half the bottle, then reminds himself to take it easy.

'I used to play here all the time,' he says, and out of nowhere hears himself telling a story about an old, dead friend. He barely notices the look of surprise on their faces. 'Bit of a sad-sack, but man, was he a great bowler,' he says.

On his next turn he gets a spear and realises it helps to talk. He wonders if that is the secret. He remembers as well to swing his arm over the middle nail; to look at the centre pin; most importantly, to hold back. Gentle is best. He knows this. He watches the ball shudder through the pins, listens to the dull crack and feels a flash of joy. Why hasn't he been back in so long? Things begin to coalesce. He is relaxed. The beer is working. He will continue to improve. He may catch Owen, if not this game, then the next.

When Tessa picks up a small, light ball he tells her to take a heavier one. Other than criticising one of her stories for a lack of balance a few weeks ago they have not spoken in weeks. He promises it will pay off. She looks at him blankly, continues with the same light ball and sinks nine pins.

Shaking his head, he checks the score again. Owen is now out of his reach, even if Dean got strike after strike.

He is the reason Owen no longer spends his nights shivering in bed, hating the rattling windows and the bitterly southerly more than he has hated anything in his life.

He sat in on the interview—for a junior role—on Barry's behalf, taking notes. Deidre, an editor in her late fifties, conducted it. He can't remember much of the interview but he remembers her flinging her arms up when Owen said something not quite correct, something balanced on the edge of poor taste; in that moment he glimpsed the large sweat patches of a tired, clever woman who grinded her whole life just to end up as the editor of the *Western Times*. In those sweat patches he saw her future: redundancy; unemployment; a quiet depression; hope in the guise of a part-time café job; incessant moaning about the state of the world, being half-listened to by a few regulars, retirees who buy their cappuccino and make it last all day by topping it up with hot water, who sit quietly by the window looking out at the traffic, wondering when life became so long and dreary ...

He saw this and realised that, though he was a few years younger, he would eventually end up in the same place.

Owen, who was subbing at the *Southland Herald* in Invercargill, was up against Marianne, a former classmate of his, a bright young woman. She was always going to get the job but Owen didn't help himself. He was desperate and, after seeing Deidre's flying arms, he came apart. He lost his train of thought. His answers were confused. At the end, in tears, he shook their hands. Deidre said he would be hearing from her. They all knew he wouldn't.

Afterwards, Dean caught the bus back to the newsroom and thought how different the city looked, how large the motorway had become, twisting and rising and growing out over the western suburbs. He wondered who was in charge.

A couple of months later he convinced Barry to hire Owen when the woman who came from advertising late in life handed in her notice after finally realising she was not going to be the next Judy Bailey.

As he recalls this, he realises Owen is thinking much the same, because he asks Dean what he did before news.

'Studied classics,' Dean says. 'But it didn't go to plan.'
Owen asks him why.
'I had a breakdown. Then I dropped out.'

Owen wins comfortably, Sophie comes second, Dean third and Tessa loses gracefully; she calls it a stupid game for children and says they should have gone to karaoke.

'Shall we make the next round interesting?' Dean says. It is like throwing a stone into a pond to see what ripples out.

He plays poker every Wednesday with a quartet of not-yet-middle-aged men—friends defined by their dread of owning a people-mover, of sleepless nights, and Saturdays spent mowing their lawn. His poker night is common knowledge; not because he ever mentions it but because he comes in late on Thursday mornings looking pale and shaky and leaves his headphones in until lunchtime.

'How much are we talking?' Owen says.
'Let's do $20.'
'Sophie? Tessa?'
'Fuck off.'

The men begin with spears. The women are forgotten. For a while the game is quiet but it gets louder. The other lane watches. Owen bowls smoothly, precisely. He is unflappable. He is a nobody in the newsroom but here in the half-light he is better than anyone. He won the first game and believes he will win the second.

Dean knows what needs to be done but his arm is not performing. He begins to yell.

'Who is this guy?' Owen says, as they watch Dean, who has never once raised his voice in the office, lose his cool. He is screaming at a bowl that veers left at the last moment.

'Fucking bullshit!' he yells. 'Get your head in the game!'

Later, over beers in a bar on K-Road, Dean tells Sophie he is leaving. Damp-eyed, he says he's reached the end of the road. His hand is on her shoulder and when she glances at it he thinks of the sub-editor, of the US correspondent, of the photographer, and tells her it's not like that. But before he has a chance to properly defend himself, Owen, who is standing on the other side of him, interrupts, and then it's too late. Sophie gets up and joins Tessa at a table on the other side of the bar, and Dean is left listening to Owen tell him it's guys like him who made him want to be a journalist in the first place.

Dean looks right through him, thinking, so this is how it ends, this is how I'm going to be remembered.

Later still, in SkyCity, when everyone but Owen has abandoned Dean, and Owen himself is so tired he feels like sinking to the carpet and sleeping right there, surrounded by the lifers, the tourists, the honeymooners, Dean asks for his twenty back so he can throw it on red and win something for the first time tonight.

Owen hands it to him. The roulette wheel turns and turns. When it lands on black, all Dean can do is laugh. He's still thinking about Owen trying to shake his hand.

He staggers down the escalator, out to Victoria Street and into a taxi. Tomorrow he won't show up. He will lie in bed, thinking of an exclusive he got a few years earlier during a murder trial in Christchurch. He will remember refusing a young, soft-voiced producer who called to ask him to go on *The Project*. He had never been on TV and said he was too busy looking after his kids. The truth was that he was afraid of the lights, the makeup, the fact it was a live recording.

Whereas in the morning Owen will stagger into the office thinking the $20 meant something, that it had solidified his place here. He won't care that Dean was particularly cold, or that he lost it, or that he had to walk home through mist and a slow grey dawn because it was the last of his money until payday. He will consider it the cost of business. He will talk to Sophie like he finally belongs. He will make his calls out in the open.

But in six months' time, when Covid begins to rumble, jolting advertisers and overseas conglomerates, he will be the first to go. Despite hitting his click quotas, he will be called into a small white room, told to take a seat, and Barry, who continues to miss Dean, who remembers what he said about Owen the day he quit, will tell him he hates this part of the job but he has no choice.

He will tell him it's effective immediately.

Owen will shake his hand. Then he will take a moment before opening the door and stepping out across the open-plan office towards his distant locker. He will think of Dean. He will know. He will remember how vigorously he slapped his hand away and he will wonder if things might have been different if he'd only let him win.

But for now, at the final drinks of the year, with only one round to go, with the scent of blood in the air, Owen has no foresight. He knows none of what's to come.

There are four pins between them. It helps that he's drunk; when he's drunk he likes to think he is a cold-hearted killer. He likes to think he will make a great reporter, that he will land important interviews with drug lords and murderers, that people will read his work. He likes to think that, like Dean, he will become a name to remember.

That's all he's ever wanted. Except tonight he also wants to win. He owes it to himself, he thinks, aligning his arm over the middle nail, staring at the middle pin. He owes it to his future to knock down every pin in a blaze of minor brilliance.

And when he bowls it is a gentle bowl, a slow bowl, and everyone watches silently as it rolls down the middle of the lane, as each pin falls steadily, inevitably, like a ripple spreading across a cold, lifeless pond. And when it's over, and Dean begins to clap, everyone winces; they shake their heads, knowingly, almost in pity, and then they begin to clap too.

GREGORY O'BRIEN

Invocation

Come the bridges over the River Clutha
  and those who cross them
Come the best and brightest fruit hoisted high
  into the air above Bannockburn
Come the resurrection of unclaimed bones
  in the hilltop cemetery at Drybread
Come the assembled tornadoes and weather systems
Come the subalpine convections, dusted and bedevilled
Come the Three Graces, Nine Muses
  and the rest of us
Come the alluvial deposit, the day bed, the shadow
  of the beloved. To speak so it might
    become words, to sing
      so it might become music.

Come the well-being of the wetlands, the restoration
  of the fens
Come the distrails and landing lights
  things as they slow or tire or sometimes quicken
    gannet fall and oyster catch, seabirds of the innermost land.

Come the diverted river, drained stream. Come rainswept
  hinterland
Come the leafage on Strode Road and Fraser Dam
Come the unstuffed mattress of this wintry sky
  the billowing sheets and night's sleep therein
Come the tailings, the compendium of
  peacocks' tailfeathers
Come ye sons and daughters of art
Come listening tree and talking leaf.

Come the ever-widening front, our singular aim
Come the wading birds, fairy rounders, the royal procession
    of quails
Come the wisdom of their governance
Come the rabbit-cluttered road to the Holy City
To sing and to be music then.

Come the streams and waterways of the Manuherikia
Come the oarsmen of Te Waka o Aoraki
Come the good morrow, the holy sonnets
Come forgetfulness, forgiveness
Come the unfinished work of every fountain
  ever built and every litre of water
       never wasted
Come remnants, heavenly chorus
Come early summer snowfall
   on sleeping forehead and water race
on hospital bed and outdoor shower—
all the shapes that are the human body.

Come calming presence, shapeless one
Come the wind down from its high shelf
Come the sun-warped clock
   on its ticking hillside, the glass hour, the time only ever
partially told.
Come the sluicings, foliage, the dancing horses and miners of Irishtown
Come the arrivals and untimely departures, and godspeed them
     across the broad, majestic Shannon
Come Italian Creek, come the roadside Spaniards,
    the Welsh underworld.
Come to all of them, in good time, the seam of golden light.
Come that gracious, unannounced moment.
To sing so everything be rendered as song.

JACKIE DAVIS

Such is the way with dreams, Simon

1.
I'm holding a syringe
attached to tubing that is connected to your heart.
I'm supposed to pull back
on the syringe to release the pressure inside you.
But such is the way with dreams,
that I look down and the barrel is now full of fluid.
Our eyes are locked
and your hand presses down on the plunger
and as the fluid enters your heart
I think that your eyes have never looked so blue.

2.
We're in a play. And we were.
Mother and son; two actors together.
I'm the governess and you are Miles.
In a Victorian coat / in a nightshirt carrying a candle.
But such is the way with dreams,
that I realised that I never got around to learning the lines,
distracted as I was with the business of raising my boys to become men.
And as you lay dying in my arms, in velvet waistcoat and short pants,
I knew the words didn't matter
but that holding your small body was everything.

3.
We're in an apartment in New York City, me and my two boys.
The TV is loud and bright; there's a pizza box on the coffee table;
the room is a cliché;
but such is the way with dreams.

Now there's a knock at the door.
I'll go, you say
and you walk the length of the narrow New York hall
and carelessly throw open the door and all I can see
is the muzzle of a silver gun in your face.
I'm so scared in my dream that I wake up.
I'm crying.
With fright, with primal terror
but mostly with relief at having woken at that moment.
Because I couldn't bear to watch you die for a third time.

PHILIP ARMSTRONG

Dualism

From the causeway we peer in both directions
across the estuary, hoping for spoonbills, whose
appearance we take as benediction.

White-robed, black-legged, black-faced,
immaculate, standing out on neutral ground,
they scythe their long blades side to side, pause
to shake headdresses into place.

Held on stilts in the bright air they delve
through clouded water into filth. What
are they after? Filthy things, which eat
and shit filth and are filth themselves.

Ceremonials complete, they roost in ngaio
trees on islets. *How do they like the taste*
I wonder. You say *that's not ours to know.*

black druid

waking too early you lie still
in feathered darkness
outside a yellow eye
pierces the black a yellow needle
sews up barbicels

himself he shakes to readiness
opens his beak unspools
his fluted thread in unrepeating
tufted loops that gather into pleats
the morning's soft-spoken material

coiling over the windowsill
his thread draws tissues
through your bony labyrinth
the night-held breath of trees exhaled
the grunts of trucks climbing the hill

puffs from the mongrel
stretched along your spine
and braided through it all
the ocean's long long ragged laces
ravelled and unravelling

MICHAEL MINTROM

View to the Alps

Dark wooden floors and hushed voices,
docents with hot-water bottles,
bells that signal time for tea.

Such details frame our days.
But where I relax on the balcony
there's the view to the alps.

In autumn the sky glows fiery gold,
fields become burnt umber
and the alps mediate between them.

I think of Van Gogh
ruminating, making worlds
with brush and paint.

Landscapes hold mysteries,
cities hold mysteries
families and bodies hold mysteries.

Nights are noisier than you'd expect,
people losing hold.
From the portico, look—

those stars, pasted onto
brushwork, tell of worlds
so close, impossible to hold.

Sound Waves from the Lost Planet

1/

Archaeologists back to the Greeks
have bickered about rubbish.
I insisted we follow the data.

Then, everything in place, we listened.
What we heard was shocking—
heavy, terrible sobbing.

2/

Starting from the Big Bang,
we collected every sound wave
the planet ever produced.

Then came analysis.
Most people don't grasp this—
the planet was silent a long time.

3/

We ripped everything apart,
squeezing meaning from fragments,
how linguists diddle words.

What caused sobbing?
Our hunch was volcanoes.
We searched for splotch sounds.

4/

Dogs and birds. Who'd believe this?
We were searching for volcanoes,
would've gone with dinosaurs

but data can't lie—
dogs barking, birds chirping
the planet's first cry.

5/

Cloud storage costs a bomb.
We chased money like bitches.
Speculation mushroomed

over the riches in our grasp.
A philanthropist enquired, could we
nab Jesus on the mount?

6/

Colleagues departed.
The lab lay bereft.
Then a breakthrough—

inside our sobs we heard
Hiroshima, Coke ads,
William Blake singing.

HOLLY BEST

Flowers

She gave the florist her real name for the card and paid with two fifties. She spelled out Rebecca's name and address slowly and importantly to the woman behind the counter, who wrote it down with a wet red hand.

'Special occasion?'

'Just for a friend.'

The dahlias, whose faces had seemed so pert and chatty, now turned their cheeks to the paper as the woman laid them down.

'Ribbon?' The woman pointed to a selection of spools.

'Navy, I think.' That would be chic, understated. Emily stuffed the change back into her coat pocket and walked out of the shop feeling tall and light, stretching her stride to cover more ground with each step. She felt like she might be in a film the way the wet street shone, the lone busker at the entrance to the station on keyboard—perhaps a Christmas film, the way the window displays glowed—and she imagined her own face bright in the sea of hats and umbrellas.

On the train she checked that the change was still in her pocket. The notes had a way of sliding out and you never heard them fall. She sat erect in her seat and tried to read her senior students' essays until the train pulled into the stop where she would change, but mostly she pretended to read, in case she missed her stop entirely or had to leap out at the last moment, getting her ankle trapped in the closing doors.

The train rushed to all the usual stops, and at one or another she thought briefly of getting off and running up the white-tiled stairwell to find the line that would take her back to the florist. The carriage lurched and an orange rolled from the bag at her feet, first forward, gaining good speed under the seats, then swinging wildly to the left and back towards her again. It was not close enough, nor was she fast enough to pluck it up as it sailed past her, and she resisted turning to see where it had got to. She glanced at the other passengers discreetly, but there was no proof it was hers, and she couldn't be seen to eat it. Though she would have considered it.

It seemed so far back now, the little florist. It was nice there, with the flowers just a bit misted and the slab of tissue on the counter all clean and ready. Emily liked the potential of it all, the way it was arranged. How the dried flowers hanging from the ceiling made you feel like you were upside down for a moment. It was a place for Mrs Dalloway, or Claudine, who would certainly send flowers to a friend. But women should send each other flowers, shouldn't they? It needn't mean anything. It was like sending a hamper if someone was ill, or a few lines from something meaningful you happened across. Yes, it was all right. They could mean anything. She wondered if they had arrived yet and were propped up by the front door. Or maybe Rebecca was filling a vase right now, plunging the stems in and watching them curtsey outwards.

She came out into the night and crossed over the footbridge, the trains reluctantly picking up speed beneath her. The platform for the Overground was quiet. An older woman in a thin beige coat was at one end of a bench seat, eyeing a man going through the bins. Emily sat down next to her. She felt like talking, felt like telling her about how she had just bought flowers for a friend. And the woman would say something like 'oh that was kind of you,' and she would smile back, proud and contained, feeling like the woman would know that in knowing Rebecca, she herself was somebody. But the momentum that had carried her out the door of the little florist and down the wet street and sucked her into the underground was gone now. As her next train pulled in, she wished again that she had sent them without a name. And if Rebecca were pleased with them, she would say well of course it had been her. Who else?

The train thudded past the familiar houses as it headed out from the city, their windows bright with lights, and people inside cooking dinner and drinking wine together, and wives setting the kindling in a pyramid before taking a match to it. She longed for the train to just keep going. She wanted to keep riding it through the night, like it was the Orient Express, winding its way to Paris. In the carriage she felt like she was outside of existence, like she was unaccounted for in the usual tick of time, and she could forget where she was going, could imagine going somewhere wonderful with wine and oysters and paté tucked under her arm.

The ticket inspector loomed above her, face like a prison guard, saying nothing. Emily checked her coat, and her bag, and her coat again, wriggled a hand into her tight jeans and pulled out her card. The woman sucked her teeth as she scanned it, handed it back, her pant legs brushing together as she moved on. Emily felt hot and wanted to get out of her coat, her armpits prickling. She rested her cheek against the cool of the window, felt it rattle the bones in her head, watched her dark eyes and pale face bobble about.

She thought of her bolshy seniors who were loud and nosey and only a few years younger than she was. Always questioning her, asking if she had a boyfriend, if she had her own place. She said she had a little flat, but really she had a room in a kind of share house. The landlady said it would have morning sun, but Emily was usually on the train before it sidled in through the curtains. Or she slept through it on Saturdays with a hangover, and the angled ceiling seemed even lower than usual. But sometimes on a Sunday she would wake with purpose, tidy up in the weak glow of the yellow room, and finish her marking with a nervous but excited feeling in her stomach as she ran over in her mind seeing Rebecca.

Rebecca had kissed her on the mouth and giggled out of the pub last Friday, her husband holding open the door. He had seen her do it, Emily was sure of it, just like he saw them cuddled together by the roadside when he pulled in to collect his wife after work. Rebecca would hop in the passenger side and give Emily a quick wave, and then the couple would be off down the road, talking to one another, and nobody else could hear them. Rebecca told Emily once that her husband had been accidentally set alight as a child while wearing a crêpe paper party hat. Emily had imagined him slapping his head with his hands trying to put out his burning crown while everyone looked on. Rebecca said it in passing, like it hadn't occurred to her that it was unusual to be disfigured like that. But Emily couldn't help thinking how strange his body must be, with patches of skin sewn on in different places.

Emily walked slowly now, up the road to the share house. She thought she might try and pinch somebody else's butter from the fridge in the kitchen downstairs, then make a run for it, make a sandwich. She had a kettle and a toaster on the windowsill in her room and a beer fridge that doubled as a bedside table, though she wasn't convinced it kept anything at the right temperature. She avoided the others in the big house. She ate little party plates of deli food perched on her bed, used the shared bathroom either very early or very late, and tossed her carefully tied bags of rubbish down the stairs before silently closing her door again. Sometimes she would just pour old pickles and yoghurt straight out the window, then aim flat soda water after it, trying to coax bits off the dormer windows below. Tonight, as she sprinkled crumbs out through the curtains, watching them drift away into the night, she couldn't stop thinking about the dahlias, their dear faces lolling on their long necks.

She saw Rebecca first thing. Saw her loose bun and black coat slip down the corridor, watched the way she balanced her stack of books on a slim hip as she unlocked the door. Rebecca looked up to find Emily leaning in the doorway. Emily flapped a little wave and said, 'How was the rest of your weekend?'

'Oh, it was nice,' Rebecca said, placing stapled worksheets out on the desks. 'Thanks for the flowers.' She looked at Emily and gave her a brief smile. 'You didn't need to do that, you funny girl.' She walked to the front of the class and started writing up an exam question as the bells began to ring.

'I know,' Emily said. 'I just saw them.' But the students were brushing past her now, shouting to one another, their shoes squeaking on the lino. She stepped back into the corridor, the rising and breaking voices bouncing louder and louder off the walls and all around her.

The boys were leaning back on two legs of their chairs and laughing when Emily walked into her own class. She put her papers down on the desk and waited as they dropped their phones into their pockets and the girls finished with their hair.

The clump of bodies compartmentalised into a grid. All except one girl, always this same girl, who talked just a sentence longer than all the others. Emily was tired of seeing her hulking shoulder twisted around to the desk behind, her shirt riding up and her body squeezing out, her one annoying voice out of time. Suddenly Emily was beside this girl, pulling her out of her chair.

'You're no more special than anyone else in this room,' she hissed at her. 'You just can't help yourself, can you?'

The girl tried to look around, laugh a little, but the teacher's face was so close to hers, so scared looking.

'Can you?' She said again. The teacher looked around the room, a peculiar expression crossing her face. She dropped the girl's arm, motioned for her to sit down.

'Does anybody else feel like talking?'

SHIRLEY ENG

Drowning the Children

I barrel my toddler
through the school pool's deep
end, in chase
of his big brother.
The baby laughs from his seat
on the edge. Their father
must be around
somewhere.
When the baby dives
into the translucent blue
his white body
drifts in slow tumble and bubbles escape
like hope in wine.
My reptile brain makes me
slow-drop the toddler and dive
to fumble the baby from the bottom.
The toddler glides down,
less elegant
than his baby brother, yet
his white-blond hair
floats a corona, or
a halo.

I find strength to grab and prop
both children up on solid ground.
Water deluges from them. More than
you'd think
such small, shivering bodies
could hold.

Gasps, coughs, blinks, shudders.
Tears wash
from me as I blot
up my sin
in their towels, and *you're all rights*.

Childhood trauma
echoes, the radio expert explains,
throughout
their lives.

Now my children are their own marred,
grown men,
I think of the other times I failed
to pay them enough
attention.
I glimpse, as I sink into a dull, dank pool,
a shape swell and urge a mother
to drive her ruined angels
off road, into a lake, a river
or smother their shallow
breathing
with a pillow.

LORENZ PÖSCHL

Ci serve un titolo (Settler Vectors)

I had never heard the name Adolf Hitler before I came to New Zealand.

It must have been a fine day in the south of '95, the south so far north, with grass and fruit scents clipping the air, and the hol(e)y radiation playing its ashen music on our hides.

I hadn't long cut cloud to come to this long land, our leprous plantain in the violent wash of Pacifica.

Through the sun-glitter, a boy of twelve called to me. A *senior*, he was geological from down here: anything he might have said would have been a mountaintop pronouncement, and his sneer chiselled me in stone-cold contours.

I—a fair child, fair-hair child, blue-eye child, an Aryanist's dream, a dream I did not know to have been dreamed: anti-eidolon, ghosting naïf through the young imaginary.

Fewest weeks prior, my father had sent me to my new school with a tiny German–English dictionary, blandished me with security. The sleeve was happy-room yellow with a bright blue logo: *Langenscheidts*, the Oxford of the 'Kraut'. Authority, Surety, Shade against the dazzling light. I could read, but the sounds—slippery centralisation of 'kiwi' beaks, to boot—escaped me. Perfectly useless, absolutely useful: my Legi-teddy. Not kitsch, form sans function, but blessing, firm trans-function: my parents' goodwill in ten thousand words with appendices.

Words were amorphous, a morph-ous am, am or for us, for *us*, more or less a house, for *us*, forming, frothing, fleeting, to hold fast the passage of the child's day, for me a house in sight, in sound the sight of speech to come. But I knew enough when he said 'We don't like Germans here because of Adolf Hitler.'

Do, do not, like: these come first, even to one who skims a language only to impress, to get laid, so forth. And the exile, the stranded, the novel, the body outta place surely learns their name, their passport vector, the first faint outlines of their whakapapa. I knew he was speaking to me, about me, about what he might have taken to be me, the nameless particular in grand generalities: anti-eidolon, young ghost in the naïf imaginary.

What does the child care for causality? Storybook, magic image, spontaneous ignition of games without rules or lines. Because is because, is cause enough, is mountaintop. Without a tongue, I had only the rest of my body. Rejection comes as a crumpled bag for the intestine, plastic bag, plasticity of body, ribcage folding into pelvis, triste Buddha: I was caught in the foreign centrifuge—get the fuge outta my centre, kid—and spun away, silent, folded, defeated in my place.

I had never heard the name Adolf Hitler before I came to New Zealand.

I had never felt the strangeness of my home.

I had never fought myself to find home in becoming strange.

I had never fought to make my home strange.

JANET CHARMAN

18 sex treats

1. sun-up—as i open the house curtains
the cat sprints behind me
to stare out every revealed view
for encircling
suitor/predators

2. can you stop him drinking?
and smoking in bed
—be honest

3. we know all about you
down to the greasiness
at the tip of your penis
—but what
really
do you know about us?

4. after so many of these tantalising
telenovelas
i awaken from a dream in Mandarin
with full understanding
—or was it Korean?

5. our nuclear-free policy
asserted from the non-smoking
section of a planet
due to be fumigated

6. look! if you have to write a review
that could substitute as my obituary
publish it when i'm dead

7. should you decide
to write a review that admits
the lesbian subtexts
of what i've said
how might i repay you?

8. and for thinking this much about sex
when i have only one breast
what is the penalty?

9. try to forget all the protein shakes
and skinless chicken breasts
that made him into her ripped love interest

10. choose a number
double it and multiply by 6
—that is the total of terribly
disappointing episodes of male gaze erotica
he represents

11. to see her rest in his arms
while she guides his hand
—for that i'd wait a long time

12. actually
how much longer will he be
by her side
as that river of alcohol
sweeps them to oblivion

13. yet when men touch each other
even in a fight scene
notice the actors who
though they don't know what
to do with it
know their desire

14. as i walk
if i scowl and swagger
i feel better

15. one of my frenemies
is at the breast-care centre
i want to speak to her
but she doesn't see me

16. twenty-nine kissless episodes in
i'm ready to get on the train to Busan
then she suggests to her fake husband
that while she makes dinner
he take an after-work shower
and he says
'help me take my clothes off'

17. lying down for a nap with
my work-wife
—she is burnt butter
i wash her
we wash each other

18. as light as sun the waiting for delight
your touch—the wind to my hat
i wind a weighting scarf
and hold you
fast

GAVIN HIPKINS

On Still Life

1. *Four Oranges*, 2022
2. *Five Limes*, 2022
3. *Four Lemons*, 2022
4. *Six Lemons*, 2022
5. *Five Lemons*, 2022
6. *Four Plums*, 2023
7. *Five Plums*, 2023
8. *Four Apricots*, 2023

All works archival pigment prints, 480 x 600mm.
Courtesy of the artist, Michael Lett and Hamish McKay.

While I have photographed a range of still life subject matter over the last thirty years, my recent turn to more traditional subjects, including seasonal fruits, signals a reappraisal of what the art historian Norman Bryson has identified as 'the overlooked'. A focus on the close at hand inevitably holds a conversation with still life painting traditions, including studies by Édouard Manet, Henri Fantin-Latour, and more recently, Gerhard Richter.

These photographs are layered with multiple exposures. The exposures are made 'in camera'—inviting chance movements. The camera itself is handheld, meaning there is an inevitable slippage across the different exposures, resulting in a saturated rendering of time and motion. These qualities magnify the spatial relationships between the individual objects. Still life studies once afforded associations of a naturalness, even wholesomeness, of the quotidian. In our age of processed food, these earlier connotations have been surpassed with a suspicion for the enhancement of the subject itself. Given its technical ability to compress time and scale, digital photography invites us to look closely at this exaggerated everyday.

—Gavin Hipkins

NICK ASCROFT

Another Poem with a Found Feather

Another poem with a tūī going nuts in a kōwhai.
Another poem with a kid, eyeballs strangled mid-epiphany.
Another poem with incongruous vocabulary.
Another with a day moon, clubbed by analogy.
Another agog at the vastness and opacity of the inner planet, the intolerable kilometres of tight hot sludge.
Another strewn with fuckery.
Another with the author spraying terror from their pupils on the kitchen window vista.
Another with a line they will unwrite, rewrite, revert and torment themselves with until dead or insensible.
Another poem of longing.
Another poem with a loose end.
Another with an end that refers too neatly to the start.
A cat.
Two ducks.
A fucking pūkeko.
The seasons—blowing—plummeting—choking on smoke—as still as a lake.
Everything half lit, everything slow, the shadows described in Latinate puffery.
Another poem shouted into the ears of this peacock ex-lover.
Another's unpunctuated bamboozlement.
Another with   empty stomach.
Another poem naming:
      Philips, Nassers, Jocastas
      people who have clearly been made up or misunderstood
      people you are supposed to know or care about
      Greeks
      terminology, nomenclature, designations
      screeches you can't unhear
      an unnameable scent.
Another poem as useless at music as a penny whistle.

CLAIRE ORCHARD

The Thing Is

Put It in the Trunk, he'd say,
meaning the Boot, of course,
and I'd manage to lie

Everything down in there,
neatly folded. Then I'd close
the Boot. Masts hold Sails

upright, are handy for
stringing Flags up too, for
signalling. We used to fly

a Pennant from our Car Aerial
but it was not the Same. It said
Coromandel. Or Something.

Anyway. I have culled many
of These. It's Nothing Serious,
Doctor, I said to her and she,

believing me, gave me Nothing
for It but Time and Attention,
which was Sufficient. The way

Armchairs are only called Armchairs
because of their Arms. Chairs without
Arms are just Chairs. We never

think of It. This is often
where the Trouble starts, from
not recalling Details such as This.

RACHAEL TAYLOR

White Noise

'I just couldn't take it any longer. You must understand, this isn't an easy city to live in. The constant noise—especially traffic: you can't go anywhere in the city and not hear traffic. Sirens, horns, thumping bass from car stereos, car alarms; not to mention construction noise. I've lived here two years and I'm still not used to it. You just hear *everything*.'

The detective wasn't buying it. She wrote something in her notebook.

'I'm going to ask you again,' she said, 'and if you could answer me directly this time. What were you doing by the river on the Drummond property yesterday when three-year-old Levi Drummond went missing?'

I'd been there before, that place by the river, by chance the first time. Early spring, nine months ago. I'd driven west out of the city. I don't know why I didn't head for the coast, but I wasn't thinking clearly then either. A relationship had ended. Not one I care about now, but at the time when it was fresh and I was thrown back, single in a new city, I was raw. My anxiety was bad—I couldn't breathe properly with the thought of it all.

I drove west, over those fucking plains that just stretch on and on. It must have been an hour or more. Anxiety turned to anger, turned to despair and held. Eventually I reached an idyllic rural landscape. Dazzling green fields, strange limestone rocks. A river, poplars. I pulled over, got out of the car and crossed a wire fence into a meadow. Private property, but I didn't care. The sound of the wind through the emerging green drew me. I had never felt an urge stronger. I needed to get to the river where the wild flax grew, and the poplars stood like cathedral pillars along the banks.

I sat under the trees for the longest time, crying my heart out. I was a pathetic mess. In my sweaty hand I held a blue heart-shaped stone bought from a crystal shop just before I met the man who just dumped me. I was superstitious about this stone; it represented my perceived happiness with this person. I stood up and hurled it into the river. The trees roared with applause. 'The future is not yet written,' said the trees, and I felt a sense of relief, of rebirth. I was no longer crying. The sound of the wind in the trees washed over me.

Later that afternoon, driving back to the city, I felt mystically recovered. Recharged.

This was why I returned to the place by the river yesterday, I told the detective. I needed to recapture the feeling, bottle its essence. I lay down and, as I dozed off, I recorded the sound of the wind in the trees—my own personalised white noise. A portal to transport me there, to emotional tranquillity at the tap of a screen, anywhere, anytime.

There was a knock on the door. The detective was required elsewhere.

'Can I have my phone back?' I asked.

'No,' she said. 'Your phone's being held as evidence.'

The police interview room was small and spartan. Two chairs and a table. A video camera in a corner near the ceiling, and a rectangular one-way mirror window. Air conditioning made a low-frequency hum, but apart from that it was absolutely quiet. A chance to collect myself and get my story straight. I had once done a bad thing, but I was past the worst. I would tell the detective that I was okay now—not great, but making progress. The detective needed to know.

My sense of recovery had been short-lived upon my return to the city all those months ago. I'd come back to the human zoo, to the chaos and noise. I discovered I was pregnant by my recently departed. He told me he wasn't interested, questioned if it was even his. I stabbed him in the eye with a blunt knife. The side of his face ran with hot red tar. He looked at me in disbelief, like he didn't deserve it, and folded to his knees before flopping onto the floor.

So my recurring fantasy goes.

In fact the loser ghosted me. I was insane with fury. I forgot all about the soothing wisdom of the trees. I felt trapped inside myself like Russian dolls. A growth within a womb within a body within a shell. I couldn't stand it. I decided to abort my unborn foetus. Yes, I made it disappear; I was guilty of that.

My depression found new lows. I stayed drunk on cheap gin—it seemed fitting. I rarely got out of bed. Couldn't make it to my job so I gave it up for swimming in my boozy fishbowl of a unit. I was a unit. In those early days of summer I barely stepped outside, and when I did, I found it overwhelming. I felt like bait, some sort of fishy entrail waiting to be devoured by a hungry predator, and they were everywhere. Days were hot, and when the wind blew from the east, so did the pungent smell of burnt trash, rotten food and decomposing green waste. Exhaust streams of cloud poured overhead. A complete sensory buffet of hell.

The external noise compounded my internal turmoil. Even with the doors and windows shut the outside world was in my head. There was no way to block out the constant invasion. The never-ending throng of kinetic rubber friction on bitumen. Motorcycle exhausts blasting, engines idling, horns blaring, trucks reverse beeping. Clanging pipes of scaffolding, demolition hammers grinding, pile-drivers pounding—the soundtrack of urban intensification assaulting my eardrums.

I felt myself slipping, falling into retrograde motion. I saw a melting world—the liquid metal and rubber collapse of cars; shimmering dreams dripping off billboards against a neon sky. I heard the gravitational warp of night-time stars bleeding down, down, their hot little cries pulling on my sugar-syrup ears. For a while my delusions detracted from the noise and I sank deeper into comfortable despair.

New people rented the unit next to mine. A couple with a small child. I heard it before I saw it. Early in the morning and late at night it screamed and wailed in a language from before history. I heard these ancient sounds on the threshold of sleep. They entered my dreams and pulled me back to a half-life of fretful, exhausted wakefulness. Cochlea snails crawled out of my ears.

Venturing out during the day, I saw the child at the large front window, pressed flat against the glass, starring out. A little critter in a terrarium. Those round black eyes, tunnels of perception stretching back to the day it was born. It was pulled up on two limbs, grasping for support, negotiating its ability to balance. A young savage in the process of being broken in. So eager to move, to get out and run wild. I poked out my tongue and the poor thing grinned back. What sort of life is the city for human beings? I wanted to set that semi-domesticated creature free.

Looking away, I pushed my balled-up hands hard into my flat belly. Thank God that one-eyed ember got the flush. That prawn, that cauliflower ear. It would have been cruel to bring new life into a world this fucking hard to live in.

It came as a surprise to find that I'd stepped back from the brink. My temporary insanity and the worst of my anxiety had passed. A few weeks into the new year I had my shit together. I returned to work. The office was a ten-minute walk from where I lived. Donning the soft cupping hands of headphones, I was able to navigate the course there and home again each day. This was progress. I was still drinking every night to knock myself out, but I'd graduated from Mother's Ruin to cheap red wine. I was functional. I could feign productivity, for a while at least.

Before midnight on Sunday, in my usual post-drunk-and-late-food stupor, close to passing out, I heard the toddler from the unit next door. The child wailed inconsolably, imitating the emergency service sirens screaming along the avenues. The cries seemed more intense than usual and went on and on. I thought to check if they needed help. I waited. It continued a while longer then stopped abruptly. I watched dark red shadows bleed across the ceiling. Dead silence. Not even the road was awake. I lay very still in my bed. Then the child started up again like a triggered alarm, screaming just as whole-heartedly as before. I was relieved to hear it and quickly caught a powerful wind of sleep.

The next morning I called in sick. I felt very sad and tired and drained of energy. I needed to switch off for a long time. The unwritten future had arrived: it was my baby's due date. I was forced to confront the consequences of my actions all those months ago. The life I'd erased. I was lost, and still grieving a better version of myself.

That long day passed, and I survived. I slept hard, and the next day, yesterday, instead of being woken at 5am by traffic and 6am by rubbish trucks and 7am by construction, I slept until 9.30 and woke naturally.

An oppressive sheet of cloud was pitched over the city, but at its wavy outer edges I could see sunlight. Beyond the city limits was a wild blue bloom of sky. I knew what I had to do.

I sat on the riverbank breathing in the scent of nature and earthy damp, and pressed Record on my phone. Leaves fell around me. They landed on the rippled water and drifted by like a living fabric, a slow-moving abstraction of autumn colour. The bright reflective surface was an upside-down mirror-world of trees and sky. An illusion. The river water was clear, and I could see beneath the picture the silent depths of underwater—the weeds and stones, the silty bed. I was lost in the detail and layers and complexity. A meditation—as close as I have ever been. I lay back and watched the stirring and drift of leaves. A bluebird sky. I heard the billow and warble of birdsong, and the fine lacework of insects at their industry. High above, the trees were whispering my mantra. 'The future is not written,' they said. It soothed me like a balm. This perfect moment. I was turning into waves of energy, blurring and dissolving into the immaculate soundscape.

'I don't know how long I was like this,' I told her. 'Everything had slowed right down. I was in a kind of trance.'

'What did you hear?'

'Just the trees and river and birds. I felt the sun warming me. I closed my eyes. I didn't intend to sleep. I hadn't felt that relaxed in a long time.'

'You claim you fell asleep?'

'Yes, I fell asleep.'

'And you have no recollection of seeing a child at this time?'

'It's hard to say—no, not seeing—I *heard* a child crying. It was a fleeting intrusion.'

'When you say "intrusion", did it make you feel annoyed, angry?'

'No, of course not. I thought I'd dreamed it. I woke up because the sun had moved behind the trees and I was getting cold. I felt refreshed, energised.'

'Go on,' said the detective.

'It was over two hours since I'd arrived and my phone was still recording. I didn't leave straight away. I put on my jacket and ate a sandwich I'd packed. Then I walked to my car and drove back to the city.'

'And you drove straight home without stopping?'

'Yes.'

'What did you do when you arrived home?' she asked.

'Nothing, really.' I looked at my reflection in the one-way mirror glass, trying to remember. 'I had some leftovers from the night before, drank some wine. I got an early night. To be honest, I was keen to hear my recording and disappear back into the peace of the afternoon.'

'And then?'

'I was almost asleep when I heard it. I thought it was the kid from next door but it was so clear in the soundscape, I was startled. I was confused at how the sound had infiltrated my white noise. I turned it off and on again—it was definitely on the recording.'

The detective pressed Play on my phone, bringing the moment back to life. Through the sounds of nature, a child in distress, bleating for its mamma like a lost lamb. I screwed my eyes shut. It lasted an excruciating few minutes before it faded, leaving only the sounds of rustling leaves and murmuring water. When I relaxed and reopened my eyes, I saw the detective studying me.

'Why did you wait until today to report it?' she asked.

'I don't know. I'm embarrassed I did that. I wasn't thinking straight. I was tired, a little bit drunk. I wish I had. But I took a sleeping pill and that's all I know.'

'Okay, so, in summary, you travelled over an hour from where you live to a rural private property where you trespassed. You fell asleep, heard a child crying, you thought it was a dream, woke up not long after—we know this because you stopped the recording there. You drove home, and that night you listened to the recording, actually heard the child again, but didn't think it important enough to phone in.'

'Yes, but I didn't know,' I said. 'You're making it sound worse than it is.'

'I'm merely relaying the facts. The sequence of events as you have told them.'

I scrambled to explain. 'This morning I was scrolling the news on my phone when I saw the headline—*Three-year-old missing in remote rural valley* or something. There was a photo of the little boy. At first I didn't make a connection, but as I read on, I realised it was the area I'd visited yesterday.'

'His name is Levi. Levi Drummond.'

Why was she pressing that point? I felt guilty enough.

'Levi,' I said. 'In the photo he was smiling, holding up a fish on the end of a rod. I suddenly had this terrible feeling. I got dressed and came down here straight away. That's the truth.'

The detective stood up and walked a lap of the small room.

'Levi went missing from the farmhouse on his parents' property yesterday afternoon around 4pm.' She checked her watch. 'It's now 11.27am. That's nearly twenty hours a three-year-old has been out there alone in the wilderness. Cold and scared—terrified. Possibly hurt. Or worse. Imagine the suffering of his parents. That sleepless night. The nightmare of losing your young child and not knowing.'

She returned to her seat and sat down, looked me dead in the eyes. 'Do you understand the pain and anguish they must be going through?'

I felt my skin bur. 'Of course I understand. I'm here, aren't I? I'm helping the investigation!'

I understood, all right, that the measure of time is unequal in loss. Unrepeatable, un-take-backable. I understood the agony of suspense and of losing time, beat by beat; the incremental count of seconds stabbing away at Levi's mother's heart. What if. What if? Is death worse than trauma? I didn't know. Looking back, how much time would I take back if only I could?

'I'm going to ask you one more time on the record,' said the detective. 'Did you engage in any way with Levi Drummond yesterday afternoon by the river?'

I shook my head. 'No. I've told you everything I know.' A heavy stone of dread lodged in my gut. 'I didn't have anything to do with Levi going missing.'

'Thank you,' said the detective. 'We have your statement. You're free to go.'

Levi was found later that day, twenty-three hours after he went missing. I read about it online. The breaking news report said he had wandered off and become lost. He was hungry and mildly hypothermic but otherwise unharmed when searchers found him huddled under a flax bush. I wondered if Levi would remember the event of his disappearance when he was older. The trauma of separation and loneliness, the threat to his safety. Would it leave a damaging mark on his innocent young life? I hoped not.

In my upstairs bedroom the low autumn sun cast rainbow swatches onto the walls through a crystal prism hanging in the window. Cars surged and boomed bass, and sirens screamed on the avenue. The banging drilling shuddering industry of progress marched on. The regular soundtrack of inner-city life.

I put on my headphones, closed my eyes and pictured myself rising upwards, into the diluted blue of late afternoon. Gliding away, across the jigsaw plains, an hour's drive from the city. I pictured Levi cuddled breathless by his family. I heard the river water flow and the majestic poplars stirring.

A lemon-white sunset.

REBECCA BALL

I said *greyhound*

                          pictured
velvet skin stretched taut over ribs
pointing children outside the school
laughing calling *skinny dog* I thought
of endless looping tracks of muzzles
collars coats the crack of a gun crowds
bustling in the stands tongues lolling
gasping for air I planned to protest
against the throwing of money
at things that run till femurs
snap till chemicals leave the
bloodstream till my racing
heart drops to a lilt of
breathe in breathe out till
my costochondral joints let go
their grip when I said *greyhound* I
meant these knotted shoulders. I
meant the beat of blood against thin
skin. A cold room, a locked door.

That Silver Sea

Someone's weighed down his grave with smooth rocks. On his headstone is a stamped steel plaque. White spots cling to the words. *I went to the woods because I wished to live deliberately.* She takes a photo, zooms in on *deliberately*, feels the sting of it in her eyes. Turns from the screen to the flaking moss on the rocks, the crouching church, robotic whine of an electric engine, yellow hills beyond.

From Port Levy Saddle the water in the harbour looks like hardening silver. They stare over it as they ease into their packs, clicking and shuffling.

Not bad, he says, standing up.

Yeah, she says. Like that Scottish lake. Up the top. Our honeymoon. Remember?

But he's off already, striding across the carpark past a wooden sign to where the track uncurls up a tussocky hill. From here the sewn badges on his pack look like bright dots bobbing in time with his gait but she knows them all: the curling yellow and white peace sign, the capital G sprouting into green leaf, the rigged-up *Rainbow Warrior* beneath a cartoon sun.

After a couple of minutes her pack settles onto her shoulders and she finds a rhythm with her boots. Squeak, thud, squeak, thud. Mouse, rock, mouse, rock. A light wind musses her ponytail. She rolls the words from the carved sign around her mouth, tastes them round and woody on her tongue. Te. A-ra. Pā-ta-ka. The top pocket of her pack, jammed with merino, forms a hard brace that forces her neck forward and down. Between that and the red peak of her cap, her vision is blinkered to the small section of track in front of her, so she makes it her world, the intersections between her boots and the grass, between schist and mud, smooth dirt and ruts gouged by water and rabbits. White threads of spiderweb woven around gorse spikes. Dart of a skink on heavy rock. Lightness and weight. Movement and inertia.

The wind sighs through the tussock, throws shadows of bare boughs like striding legs onto the path. The bank climbs beside her and the trapped sunlight gives off a taut warmth. She points out a darting rabbit, hears only whispering breeze in response.

The path rises under her boots and she turns to her breathing, counts out syllables with her steps. De. Lib. Er. At. Lee. De. Lib. Er. At. Lee. She's so focused on the rhythm that she doesn't notice he's stopped at the top of the slope. Her nose smashes into the rigged-up *Rainbow Warrior*, the taste of dusty canvas in her mouth.

Sorry. She rubs her nose, checks for blood. Could've sworn you were—

Was what.

Nothing. She takes off her hat and falls back into the bank of springing tussocks, lets them take the weight of her pack before unclipping the chest brace, easing her shoulders out of the straps and standing up.

Wind bites cold on the sweat of her back, threatens to lift her up, sling her down the valley. Unblinkered, she can see the whole vista in motion. A giant whirring machine, tussock undulating in rhythmic waves. Dark swabs of gorse churning and twisting in unison, each one dotted with the bouncing white flags of spider nests. At the floor of the valley a river of sheep surges across a yellow field, tight behind the red quad, flowing back in symmetrical braids. Further up the ridgeline even the sky moves, grey mist rolling up and over the peaks, corkscrewing over the crest like a lolling taniwha. Just below her, a harrier hawk draws endless circles in the sky. She closes one eye and tries to catch it between her thumb and forefinger. Imagines it squirming in her grip. This whole world slowing to a stop without this circling bird at its centre.

The only things that are still are the grey tree stumps like broken headstones in the shifting tussockland. Them and the water, standing silver in the distance.

She clears her throat. Meant to be a giant under that water.

What.

A giant. In the harbour. I read about it. Pretty sure Māui threw him in there, loaded him up with rocks to hold him still.

Huh. Wish he'd done the same to the dickheads that cut down all those. He sweeps his hand across the stumps. Slash and burn. Jesus.

He pauses for a moment, reaches into his shorts pocket for what she assumes is his phone to take a picture of the view. Before she can register what's happening, he's flicked out the blade of his Swiss Army knife and buried it deep in one of the cottony spider nests in the gorse at their knees. He leaves it in there for a moment and when he draws it out a teeming stream of tiny spiders follows, pouring like water into the stones and dirt at their feet and fleeing into the grass.

For a second he looks at the ruined nest, flapping open and empty in the wind, then grabs his pack, slinging it hard onto his back. Carabiners clang. The ring of them in her ears as he strides away.

As they walk up the ridgeline the mist flows down and they meet it midway. The wind starts to gust. He's out of sight already and her world shrinks again, to the space between her and the next orange track marker materialising in coloured pixels from the grey, the next thrashing bush of gorse, the next bobbing spider nest. Every minute or two she hears a sound behind her, a heavy sole scuffing a twist of gorse root, the gravelly clear of a throat, shuffle of oilskin, sounds that blend with the wind and bind into a new truth—him behind her, pacing the path in her slipstream. When she shucks a bar of chocolate, she snaps it in half, holds out four dark squares behind her. It's only when he doesn't take it that she turns, teetering under her pack, and sees nothing but grey mist, dark shadows of leaning gorse.

She picks up the pace until she can make out his bobbing silhouette ahead. As she watches, a huge shadow appears in front of him, a swaying giant in the mist, and her stomach turns. She runs to catch up, takes a breath to cry out, then realises it's trees—a pair of tōtara that have been fused by the wind into one leaning body of dark leaves, two legs set in knotted wood and bark. She gets out her phone, takes a photo of him as he strides under it. His head is down, muscular calves flexing beneath his pack, and as he turns down the path to the hut she wonders how many photos like this she has of him, and whether she has ever seen herself from this angle.

The wet air has slicked the downhill path into a rutted slide. The rustling gorse closes in and stammering pīwakawaka dart in and out, twitching their striped tails and hopping from foot to foot on barbed branches. She stops to look at one, holds out a finger to it, rigid and reaching. For a second or two the wind stops, as if someone tall is standing next to her. There's warmth, like a hand on her hair, and the scrub teems with birds—tomtits, bellbirds, more fantails—all flitting to and fro, whistling and tutting, shifting and flicking through the tangled branches.

Under her boots the slick has gathered, and when she takes a step it begins to flow, nudging into the ruts carved by earlier streams and tumbling over itself down the hill.

Crazy, huh, she calls. He's ahead again, and a gust snatches at the words. What.

She yells this time. Water. How it always finds a w—

Her left boot slides on a patch of slick and her leg skids forward and out like an ice-skater's. Thrown off balance, her pack pulls her backwards and she lands, heavy, on top of it. A pain sears through her knee, making her take a yawning gasp of the shifting air.

Shit. Stop. She calls in the outbreath of her gasp, looks down the stretch of path in front of her, how it disappears into the grey in just a couple of metres.

Stop. She calls louder, braces her knee with her hands, feels the flow of water bubble in and around her backside, soaking instantly through her leggings and into her underwear. She purses her lips and breathes out slowly into the wind, bowing her head to the mud and water.

A pīwakawaka hops onto the path, starts skipping around her boots, scanning hopefully for unearthed insects.

Stop. She's quieter now, as if speaking to someone right beside her. Why doesn't he stop.

The pīwakawaka cocks its tiny head to sky, to ground, sky and ground, like it's trying to stitch them back together.

It takes him about fifteen minutes to get back to her, braced and shivering where she fell. He's packless.

Shit. I didn't realise you weren't behind me. What've you done.

She wipes the back of her hand over her eyes, feels it leave a muddy streak across her face. My knee. I'm okay as long as I don't move. Think I twisted it.

Hut's only a hundred metres down there. Gimme your pack. I'll come back for you.

Wincing, she unclips, squirms out and sits up so he can pick up her pack out of the slurry. He swings it, dripping brown, onto his back and his bootsteps disappear again into the mist.

The sudden weightlessness sends a stab of panic through her gut and she has to stem a desperate cry with her muddy right hand. She pulls out her phone again, jabs her finger at the screen. It opens onto the photo of him striding under the leaning giant. She swipes it away, lands on the shot of the gravestone, still zoomed in on that weathered steel plaque. The wet air mists up the screen and the etched words blur and refocus under her finger. Deliberately. Because. Essential. Teach. Die.

Her eyes burn and she zips the phone back into her front pocket, tries to remember words, other words, the warmups their drama teacher used to make them do. *Red leather, yellow leather. Red leather, yellow leather. Silly Sally swiftly shooed seven silly sheep. Silly Sally. Silly Sheep.* Te. A-ra. Pā-ta-ka. Te Ara Pātaka. A sound behind her, the quick *ziiip* of a shoulder strap being yanked tight, makes her gasp and she clamps her hand back on her mouth. She looks around for pīwakawaka but it's only the shifting bush, the rolling mist, the tumbling water running through and beyond her, pulling at her boots, its endless journey down and across and out to that silver sea. She releases her hand from her mouth like a valve and a low moan flows into the wind.

This time she hears his coughing before his boots. His face is red, eyes hard.

Right, come on, he says, bracing his boots either side of the track, standing tall over her. He raises his right arm and she wonders for a moment if he's about to hit her. But he crooks it down and she grabs hold, levering up on her good leg, letting out a scream as her left foot lightly brushes the ground.

Okay. Get on. He bends double and she makes one final push forward, a fumbling leap onto his back that makes them both swear and hiss. He reaches back to lock his hands under her soaking arse.

Think you're lighter than your pack, he jokes, but her eyes are closed and she's counting each breath, biting her lips, salt and metal on her tongue.

They move slowly, two bodies on two legs, leaning into the wind. She starts to count his steps, finds herself whispering in time with them, de, lib, er, at, lee, de, lib, er, at, lee, but there's another whisper in her ear, same syllables, same rhythm, and she loses track of sounds, who's saying what. When she opens her eyes to see the hut emerging through the darkening mist she isn't sure whether it's real or a hallucination, like the ghost of water on a hot road.

The hut opens into a small bunkroom with a narrow set of wooden stairs leading down to a heavy fire door. He steps down slowly, then turns around, uses her back to push open the door, then swings them both into the lounge. The door closes behind them with a dull thunk and the air's so still she can feel it hard against her cheek. There's a black potbelly, two wooden dining tables, two blue squabs propped against heavy sills. He pushes one over with his boot and eases her down onto it. She lies locked on the mattress while he gets the potbelly on, shuffling in and out of the hut with armfuls of kindling and then bigger hunks of pine. He boils the kettle, prepares two pots of noodles. They eat in silence, watching steam curl into the darkening room.

When they've finished, he rises arthritically, rinses the pots with the rest of the kettle water, pours red wine from a steel canister into them. He pushes one across to her and sits on the other side of the table.

What we gonna do, she says.

Stay put. Just gotta wait for the weather. We'll move tomorrow. He swigs from his noodle cup.

How … She doesn't finish, and he doesn't ask for more.

So there he is. He nods at a framed photo of a bearded man on the wall above her. The man wears a floppy green hat and smiles at something just past the camera. His hair is the colour of tussock.

The man who wanted to live deliberately.

What.

Nothing.

Was he the last. He takes another swig.

What.

Rod Donald. Is there anyone else left. Look at us, we can't even walk to his hut without fucking it up. We're useless. He tips the cup back, then knocks it light and hollow on the tabletop.

The wind throws branches at the windows. Inside the potbelly something cracks, a ball of sap exploding under pressure. The lounge air seems to thicken against her skin. I wouldn't call us useless, she says. We do stuff. The E-Can protest. Cathedral Square. We were there.

C'mon, that was ten years ago. And nothing's changed. You saw it today. Fucking ravaged. Gorse and rabbit holes. A couple of stunted tōtara. It's fucked. He refills his cup, drinks again.

What about sustainable farming, though. Zero emissions by 2050. The words hang in front of her, take new shape in the stiffening air.

How many years has science has been telling us what to do. But we didn't. I've tried to do stuff. To move things forward. But for what. May as well just sit back and get drunk. He raises his noodle cup to the tussock-haired man, presses it dully against hers, leaves a gnawing dent in the recyclable plastic.

In the white light of the camping lantern, her preparations are suddenly ridiculous. Compostable ziplock bags. Solar cellphone charger. Scroggin. The pinot pounds nauseatingly in her head and she's suddenly desperate to get away from this still air, the cracking fire, lines of pots and bags, enamel and steel.

Ready for bed, she croaks.

He drains his cup and picks her up, making a seat for her with his interlocked hands, letting her legs hang limp on either side of him. Outside he helps her pull down her leggings and makes another brace with his arms for her to lean into while she pisses. She has a thought that she should apologise but before she can speak the wind and dark whip it all away. Between the grass slashing her feet and the trees thrashing above her there is nothing else to hear.

Inside, he lays her, wincing and shivering, on a low bunk bed. She takes a quick gasp of cold air as he straightens out her leg.

Should be okay here. Only hurts if I move it. She lets go of the words with an outbreath, feels them lukewarm on her chin.

Silently, he fashions her a splint out of two rolled-up travel towels, presses them either side of her knee. He goes to slide her sleeping bag over her legs but she yelps, so he unzips it and drapes it over her.

More, she breathes, shuddering, and he empties out the rest of the clothes from the pack on top of her.

All right, he says, patting the pile, his touch flat through the layers. I might sleep downstairs. Let you get some rest.

Can you … she starts but he's already gone, dull thump of the fire door behind him.

Her knee sears. She focuses on being still. The wind picks up another branch and drags it over the roof. She hears the distant clang of steel as he replaces the lid on the empty canister. Pictures him at the wooden table, hand locked on his noodle cup, eyes fixed on the green-hatted man.

She closes her eyes, sees the slow spread of moss across those rocks on his grave, slow bite of white spots into words etched in steel. Live. Deliberately. Te Ara Pātaka, carved in wood. Those trees bent double on the skyline, the undulating tussock, the twitching fantail, the harrier hawk squirming like a baby mouse between her thumb and forefinger. Death roll of a taniwha on the ridgeline. White flags in the wind. Water. Falling, running, carving ruts into dirt and schist, pooling, setting. She crosses her arms around her chest, feels the weight of organic merino, woven hemp, sustainably sourced bamboo. Imagines they are a silver sea pushing her into a soft bed of harbour mud. Moss-covered rocks into velvet soil.

NICOLA THORSTENSEN

Transmutations

The vague remains of the castle you and I crafted
in wet sand below the high-tide mark.

A spider's fretwork
you swept away during spring cleaning.

Your quick craftsman's hands
which coaxed this desk from a timber slab.

This room, two walls into its makeover, waiting for you
to apply paste to the next length of paper.

Your falsetto rendition of 'Hey Big Spender'
that brought the house down, hushed,

your hands now at rest across your chest,
as if cast in grey plaster.

CINDY BOTHA

Stung

A paper pomegranate has sprouted
from the fence: a wasps' nest seeded
with larvae, defended
by a seethe of wings—
I came too close, one tiny sniper
took me down. The pain's surprising

but, as my fingers flush and swell,
I'm beguiled: worn posts pulped
and sculpted to a papier-mâché citadel
with guards at the gate.
I imagine a tang like frankincense,
the scuff of almost-wings

as gluey pupae flex in the brood-cells.
A sentry shifts,
interrogating my position, tight-belted
warrior, shivering her tawny hips—
bent on seeing me off. One hand's
a crude balloon-animal, or I'd applaud.

RACHEL SMITH

if a star explodes on a distant ceiling who will see the light

She tells me to go the quick way, down the road and along the path that cuts through the old cemetery, where we went on a school trip last week and took pencil rubbings of gravestones and she cried at the little grave down the back because her baby brother had been found dead in his bed ten days before.

She tells me not to stop at the park, even if the other girls are there having a smoke and a laugh and squeezing their fat arses into the kids' swings; go straight to her house and find the key under the big rock beside the letterbox, let myself in, she'll be there soon.

She says all this as the last bell goes, the two of us moving out the door and down the steps, says it as if it's what we do on a Friday night on the first day of summer. I nod, like you do when your best friend's brother died and you don't know what the fuck to say, when the only thing you *do* know is that the words your mum wrote in a card with a white lily on the front—*condolence, sorrowful, sympathy*—are the wrong shape to fill a brother-sized hole.

I let myself in, walk quiet past her mum's closed bedroom door, read a magazine until she comes home, slides through the window on her belly and topples onto the floor. She sits cross-legged on the bed, opens her bag and takes out nail polish she pinched from a shop.

She paints my nails and tells me some bullshit story about how she's going on a trip overseas next month, somewhere far from here with a beach and a theme park. I nod, like you do when you best friend's brother's ashes are in the room next door, tell her the blue polish will look best when she's lounging poolside.

Later, we lie on her bed—toes, hands and heads touching—play that game where we hold our breath and stare at the glow of stickered constellations on her ceiling, count the stars exploding in our eyes.

DEREK SCHULZ

Kō

From *élan vital*

There was a steeple in the distance with a flag hoisted to half-mast so when the bell began to peal I thought it might be Sunday but it wasn't. Nowhere near. It was a Friday, early morning with the town set to open, then make its way out to the end of yet another day. That bell must have been Mrs Palmer's rather giddy grandfather clock, located in the hallway downstairs. It only ever chimed out for half past eight, be it am or pm, and as I cautiously pulled at those studio curtains to try to figure what exactly might be going on, Kō, with an effortless swing, came down the steps of the old Herald building in her shade cap, tank and white shorts, camera slung over her right shoulder. I watched her lope up the street and disappear into someone else's story—the blonde hair and spartan caste of her. How easy she made it look.

Buy Now, Pay Later

What appears to be a simple folktale is the huia shop next door. There were half a dozen fresh ones hanging in the window alone. Then a tame little thing caged at the back of the shop, waiting to be plucked at her maturity. She is a bold drawcard because te huia i Tararua have a simple, trustful nature. They come when you whistle so you can go up into those back hills and knock out three or four hundred at a time. Puerile fancy aside, there isn't a piece of them can't be turned into cash. Fed up on pūriri berries for free, there's at least as much meat as a miromiro, which can be skinned and cooked to your choice in the little spit oven on the counter—wattles off or on. The skin is then stretched and turned toward a fire. Once dry it can be stitched into a purse or wallet, or any couturier-like thing, while you wait. The feet having been removed, you leave the shop with one on a silver chain, charmed around your neck. They give you the second to put on the internet. Olive oil lube will keep them working for at least another month, to encourage better luck. This is all from the brochure. I had stopped eating and begun longing for my last 40 minutes to end so couldn't get in there myself, but their world had become an oyster. They're exporting to Paris, Berlin, Milan and beyond, with all the top museums begging for a stuffed couple to set beside a moko'd māhuna. This has been corroborated by many corroborating statements.

STEVEN TOUSSAINT

A Quidam

Pity one can't pretend
The studied otherness of a jobber.
Some people sit on their hand,
A game they call The Stranger,

Or so I am told. Competitive
When it comes to guessing the next whim
Of an imperial favourite,
Here I queue to beg of him

Expensive imprimatur.
In the pop-up shop beside the taco van
Shrug and pert non sequitur
Are modest comfort to the also-ran

Exhausting silver whippets in the park.
I hear the tinkle of an empty canister,
Tiny 'Greensleeves' in the dark.
The Boomer I become will answer,

Is there really such a thing
As a clean hand? In time, they will assign us
Noms de guerre ad hominem
Like Juvenal Aquinas.

An American

An American, for my sins,
I can't authentically mourn the dead of World War I
Like our British or Kiwi cousins,
Buttonholes on fire with plastic Eyes-of-Sauron.

Inveterate Anywhere, I can hardly admire
Sir Peter Jackson's uncanny vale
Of misery, where respectively teach and tower
Holograms and Anzacs-to-scale

Beneath obligatory silver fern.
They make me feel, somehow, that grey power won.
Formidable belligerents, taciturn
Till the last evicted Took is bussed away from Hobbiton.

JOSIAH MORGAN

Overhaul

Cider eyes! The man of the belt is no longer!
Chrysalised! No longer statued! Not Leontes' wife!
The pilgrim! The traveller! No longer in one place!
Reflowering! Feeling! Cider eyes! Cirrus, overcome!
The seasons change! Barefoot!
Drizzle the vinaigrette on the salad!
Susurrate the leaves! He's well adjusted! Climate conscious!
Pays his carbon credits! Rings the bells! Sounds the sirens!
Votes like his parents! Threw his dirty books away!
Nimbostratus, abate! The siren scalpelled the fear away!
Cider eyes! Cumulus, hurrah!
Bird shit! Dog ear! Cider eyes! Cider eyes!

PHOEBE WRIGHT

Heart of Gold

Jez often thought about killing her clients. Maybe it was the years of deciding, in one glance, whether she could take them, what she could use as a weapon, how she'd get to the door. Maybe it was a natural extrapolation of a dom's prerogative. But it wasn't subs she thought of killing. It was the simpering 'Girlfriend Experience' clients. The ones who wanted her to dress in casual clothes. Wear what you wear to yoga. Wear your PJs! Go easy on the makeup. It was the ones who wanted it to feel real.

It'd be simple to do. There were pillows, and every bed and massage table had hand and foot cuffs attached underneath. She poured drinks in a cameraless room where she could easily stash a bottle of something less palatable behind the wigs. And she was strong, if it came to that. She went to a combat-themed aerobics class three times a week. Fantasised, as she kicked and punched and did push-ups amid the lycra and swinging ponytails, that they were a secret army preparing to infiltrate brothels across the land and take out a hundred johns in a night.

She'd do it when she was ready to leave anyway. Pack up her lingerie and makeup, carefully clean or steal anything else with her DNA on it. Occasionally there was a day when she had appointments back-to-back. If no other girls were in, Sal would slip away to go to the gym or whatever else she did in the tiny windows of time when she wasn't at Babylon. Because Jez was totally trustworthy and could deal with any ugly mug. That's how Jez could take more than one life.

Steve with a pillow to the face, his thin old-man arms flailing. Doug with a vintage cast iron bondage stock to the head (he was big—surprise would be the way). Andy with a belt across the throat while his stupid guns strained uselessly at the cuffs. Leave Sal to find them, be long gone. No one at Babylon knew her real name, or address, or the account in which she deposited her wads of cash. Or any contact details beyond a phone she bought specially for work, which she would throw in the sea. No one knew she worked there.

Some girls couldn't help themselves. They told friends and flatmates, thrilled at the drama of coming out. One girl told her crush so he would want to save her from it all. Such bullshit.

It occurred to Jez she could be a more prolific killer if she went independent. She didn't love the idea of throwing Sal under the bus with a scandal. Sal was a decent boss, as pimps went. Jez could make a different profile each time, conduct icy, perfect exterminations in every posh hotel in the capital, then hit Auckland. Only revenge for what many, many men have done to hookers, in life and in so many stories. So let them fear. Let them scrutinise every escort page for signs of madness, weigh up their lust with their dread.

Arguably she'd be damaging her colleagues' business. Delilah always shuddered when she said 'colleagues'. Reckoned there was some kind of sacred sisterhood. Sal always said *The girls*, *You girls*, and Jez knew she had to think how the clients did, but wanted to spit *We are women*. If that. Jez's relationship with gender was mercenary. She always said *She*, *Her*, with a resigned shrug. Didn't know what to think. But one thing she did know: hookers everywhere would be secretly stoked if someone out there, even just one time, took out a john.

So when Sal told Jez she would be seeing Michael, a sixty-nine-year-old in need of an erotic massage with a happy ending who wanted a more experienced sex worker because he had an implant in his shoulder, Jez froze, one hand groping in her locker.

Sal barrelled on, folding towels. *If ya press it the wrong way it could stop his heart! Scary eh!*

Jez pulled her suspenders and makeup bag out of the locker very slowly. Yeah. Scary.

Didn't seem interested in extras, sorry to say.

See about that.

Jez had her tricks for getting extras out of tight jerks. She'd lean close, bite her lip, kiss his cheek, whisper, *So, you into kissing?* Fifty bucks if so. She'd straddle him backwards, naked on the massage table, ostensibly to rub down his legs, flexing her bare everything in his face until he stammered, *Can I ... am I allowed to touch you?* Fifty bucks. She'd angle him neatly at the last moment so he came on her tits, whether he wanted to or not. Fifty bucks. You get the idea.

Jez yanked on a g-string with superfluous layered straps that arched over her hips, a matching bra that left more tit uncovered than covered, a translucent black mesh dress over top, and seven-inch black spike heels.

Delilah was fussing with a low ruffly neckline, making sure the girls were just about busting out. Said, *You know Michael isn't a dom appointment, right?*

Jez surveyed the terrifying mirror with satisfaction. *Yeah, that's why my undies are bloody pink.*

Del wore classic makeup, perfect curls, and always a cocktail dress. Trad fem. Boring. Sal wrote '40s film star' on Del's profile, '60s pixie' on Alexa's, using eras and anything else at hand to pull attention away from the fact that almost all of them were skinny or skinny-adjacent middle-class Pākehā, probably pretty interchangeable if it came down to it.

Jez poured Michael's wine in the storeroom, and Diet Coke for herself. She marketed on hard, lean lines and her metabolism didn't cooperate as well as it used to. Plus, any little thing you can do to have more control than them, do it. She slapped her smile back on as she reentered the massage room.

Michael sipped the chilled wine. *You want to know why I chose you?*

Desperately.

He clocked the sarcasm and smiled. *Your name. My boat's called Jezebel.*

Weird name for a boat. She was thinking, if you have a boat, you can afford extras. Turned out he lived on it. Docked at the waterfront, sailed free all around the islands. His face was weathered. Jez couldn't immediately find anything to hate about him, which was not usually a problem.

So what do you do on your boat?

Turned out they were both readers. He was surprised someone her age would like Steinbeck, and Jez bristled and recited the opening lines of *Cannery Row*.

His forehead sprang into grooves like seabed sand when he laughed. *You could write something like that. About this place.*

Jez snorted. She normally hid her very snorty laugh, with johns. *I'm not a writer. Plus who'd read that? People who buy books are nice ladies who belong to book clubs and drink lattes in the morning and Mud House wines at night. Trust me, no one hates us more than nice ladies.* She glanced at the clock. *You better get in the shower.*

While Michael was in the shower Jez arranged the massage oil, lube and towels, stripped off the dress, kicked off the heels and adjusted straps in the mirror, rolling her eyes about the Cannery Row thing.

Michael came back with a towel around his waist. His chest was leathery with freckles and wiry-skinny. She could see the implant, sticking straight out from under his collarbone. She glared away from him and said, *Babylon Brothel in Te Aro in Wellington is a candied castle, an old joke, a cum stain, a heartbeat, an origami woman made of twenties, a Russian roulette, a bad habit, a black hole.*

Michael leaned his head back and ditched the towel. His penis hung matter-of-factly in its place, the size of a lighter. He said, *Babylon's inhabitants are whores, madams, ugly mugs and motherfuckers. Or enlightened nuns, dashing rogues, and angels of death. Or something.*

Jez stared at him. Then turned away abruptly, chugged some Coke, and came back with a tight smile. *Lie on your front first. Let's just see how we go with extras. I love spontaneity.*

She worked oil into his calf muscles, which stuck out like tennis balls under his scaly skin. Up the thighs, prising buttocks apart, appreciating that, unlike many men, he'd had a good clean in there. He moaned as she worked his shoulders, taught as pulled ropes. Jez stripped off, squirted oil in a zag across her body and climbed up, breast sweeps and body slides, taking satisfaction in his involuntary sighs.

Roll over.

Yes, ma'am.

She stood looking not at his erection but at the rectangle of risen skin under his collarbone. He sighed, looked at her the way so many people want to be looked at, and put his palm to the side of her tit as gently as you'd cup a child's face.

So tell me about the implant. I don't want to fuck this up.

He took his hand off her and moved it to the implant. *It releases medication into my blood.*

Sal said it could kill you.

This is how you'd do it. Press here and hold. Like a button. He laughed. *This is how you unplug a man.*

So easy.

Imagine if more women had their fingers on such switches.

Why would you show me that? I could have just avoided the area.

There was something in his eyes, then. They looked at each other for longer than anyone usually does, in the industry or out of it. Jez abruptly turned and started on his quads, flirting up around his inner thighs, nudging balls. His dick strained up, and up again, trying to find something that wasn't there. Erect, it was the size of a small zucchini. It looked so earnest. Like it was about to burst into tears.

I could go anytime anyway, doctor says. I told Sal as much.
What?
What if I'm ready? What if you could be my angel of death?
Jez scoffed.
You're angry, he said. *It might make you feel better.*
You're smarter than some of them, aren't you?
What do they do? Believe your smiles? Invite you out on their boats?
Are you inviting me out on your boat?
Michael laughed. *I'm not under the illusion you'd spend unpaid time with me. I'm smart, remember.*

And somehow Jez was filled briefly with sea air, and what it would be like to be on his boat, cross Cook Strait, trail her fingers in luminescence, wake up surrounded by jellyfish big as dinner plates. Wear jeans and a jacket over comfortable, practical undies, hear him tell the stories that were soon going to be lost to the world forever.

She shook her head free of the image and filled her hand with lube before grabbing his dick, much the way a Subway worker grabs the mayo tube. She'd forgotten to push him for extras.

You wanna go out with a bang?
I was told strictly no sex in the massage rooms.
Well, it's also strictly no murder, but you went and asked for that.
Another look, his sea-grey eyes flickering as her hand moved up and down, chin tilting up like the prow of a boat.

Jez didn't even think about it. She reached for the condom drawer, ripped one open with her teeth and climbed on top of him.

Tell me about the boat. Where will we go?
And Michael told her, halting and gasping, about sounds, secret islands, Spirits Bay, deep Fiordland, the wild West Coast, abandoned shacks, dolphins, humpbacks, sunfish, the Pacific, reflected stars, infinity above and below.

Jez rode a little harder and asked with her eyes.

Michael gave a little nod and reached for her face and then her hand, put her finger on the side of the implant. She could feel he was about to come. He pulled her close and moaned into her hair. She felt him shudder and buck and squeezed hard—both pelvic floor and her finger and thumb on either side of the implant under his skin.

Michael's eyes went glassy while his cock still heaved. Jez climbed off very carefully. His body flopped in place, still dribbling. She stood over him shaking and then, on muscle memory, cleaned him up with a small towel and wrapped herself in a big one. That one part of him still looked alive. She remembered reading somewhere about angel lust.

He'd left a stack of notes by the drinks. Jez stuck it under her sweaty boob and told Sal he died on her and that he had been going to pay by card.

Jeeesus, Sal said. *That's all we bloody needed today. You all right, doll? Look, take a bottle of Mud House home. Watch something stupid and forget about it, okay? He died happy.*

Jez dressed numbly and slipped out past the flashing lights of the ambulance. She walked to the waterfront, drinking straight from the bottle, knowing no one would say shit, not even a cop, because of the stink of fearlessness and life pouring off her. She drank the whole thing, walking around the boat docks, looking and then asking for a boat called *Jezebel*. No one had heard of it. She finished the bottle, thought about putting a message in it, but didn't, and threw it into the sea.

BRETT REID

White Irises

Yesterday, without warning,
across the street from our house,
petals fanned out, towered bright in the sunlight.
Then last night they caught the streetlamp's dull eye
brought to mind the low-lumened floodlights
of the local football club's practice pitch
where on pitch-black winter nights
in the farthest corner
the less well-honed get relegated,
so heads meet crosses inflated with stone.
Iris flowers live a few days. Not long to shine.
Names pop up. Jim, Janis, Jimi. Mama Cass Elliot.
There's a shrine where Marc Bolan died.
Fresh flowers get left all the time.

JENNIFER COMPTON

Within the Room

After 'Snow' by Louis MacNeice

I am considering the architecture of this 12-line poem.
Do you know it at all? And if you do, did it catch your fancy?
Is it a sonnet, maybe, that refused to understand itself?
There is a capital letter at the beginning of each line—

Like they used to do back in 1935 between the Wars I and II.
Did he spit the pips of the tangerine into the spiteful fire?
Which is also gay: sometimes a word will accrue meanings.
I hope I have used the colon correctly. A colon is so sudden.

The roses are pink and they are huge in the great bay window,
And here is the hinge—against the glass, snow is spawning.
How is that even possible? Inside the room a fire and a tangerine,
and roses: outside, winter. There has been a hothouse on the scene.

KERRIN P. SHARPE

Te Hau o te Atua/The Breath of Heaven

1
Ōtamahua Quail Island long widowed
by ponies and dogs never used to living alone
stuck at home behind windows of tarutaru
fringes of toetoe watches stables split
and cup in the southerly watches rust
gnaw sledges bits and bridles watches neglect
collapse dog kennels still finds old stitches
of hoof and paw tilt Her towards the stout
heart of Antarctica

2
to get to sleep Rebecca relives walking
around Ōtamahua past the dog kennels
to Ivan Skelton's cottage down to his grave
at South Point its slim waist of gritty soil
its Lord's Prayer in a plastic coat its lonely
white cross ... over the hill to the Ships'
Graveyard their bones rocking in loose
steel jackets ... down to where conger eels
rise from the dusky sea slither up sharp cliffs
through wet feathery grass to wait in
the stagnant pond her father ... *hurry
Rebecca if you miss this ferry you'll have
to stay on the island ... the island*

3
ponies pull Scott and Shackleton around
Ōtamahua in wheeled sledges their iron
harness keeps them in line helps them steer
the ropes and laws of ice makes them heroic
mauled by frost hauled by moons they grow
manes of toetoe hooves of basalt in the cold-hearted
darkness they lie on their backs and name seabirds
ring-billed gull red-billed gull taranui they run
to Walkers Beach where fallen pines puncture
the sea they run to Saddle Gully through tassels
of wind though they leave for Antarctica (there are
photographs) they never leave here

4
under the eaves of the leper's hut on Ōtamahua
swallows spin the mouth of a nest trumpets
of swallows low and fearless all day their cup
fills their cup empties handfuls of swallows
all hush and tremor swallows as light as the only
leper in their care Ivan Skelton confined by his
own skin hears even in sleep the sea weave a path
towards his father in Apia towards his mother
whispering into shells hears now her sudden fierce
change from longing to lament and lurches awake
the door's open the swallows inside massive in moonlight
their shadows a carousel on the rough pine walls each
swallow each swallow each swallow raising its wings
like oars bursting into light blessing Ivan just as the Tulafale
blows the conch

5
some afternoons clouds sweep and baste Ōtamahua with
sun till the island illuminates dog and pony tracks Ivan's hut
his grave the shallows where ships sleep each time Sheryl
passes Ōtamahua she remembers stories of waves that stole
the young farmers Henry and Edward from their boat
in Wards Bay in her sleep their eyes light a pathway through
Te Whakaraupō Lyttelton Harbour light the waka that carries
them home

6
the Antarctic explorers leave Te Whakaraupō Lyttelton Harbour
the slap slap of waves like sorry like sorry they sail their wooden
rooms in the mouth of a re lent less rolling sea even after
the warm karakia the salutes hooters hats in the air the most
peculiar songs of ponies they become distant shawls of bone
sliding one ski in front of the other travelling towards ice
that may never release them even as they follow the compass
from waters deep to pastures white someone here with
frozen breath and muslin hood writes

    plant toetoe harakeke tarutaru
    to shield Ōtamahua from
    shadows /of /ice

7
Bill's Cabin returns tongue-and-groove unused from Antarctica
man-hauled up Clifton Tce planted in Kinsey's garden Te Hau
o te Atua The Breath of heaven a chapel for Oriana Wilson
who prays for months the ice sends the doctor home Our Lady
of the Snow/Star of the Sea a bedroom for Kathleen Scott who
knows the doctor and captain lie frozen beneath the Ross Ice Shelf
who finds in the garden Scott's messages we have slept here/think
of me and sketches snow petrels offering them to the sky in one
long sad song a kennel for the husky Osman the Great to remember
the wave that swept him off the *Terra Nova* and the wave that

swept him on again a shanty marooned in wood holding its jarrah
anchor in seismic rages Bill's Cabin now @ Godley Head watching
Ōtamahua still destined to wait hearing in the wind the sorrows of ice
    weave a kete
    fill it with
    Waiata /for/waiting

8
in all weathers the bronze sled dog stands on the corner
of London and Canterbury Streets looking across to Ōtamahua
waiting for the captain's whistle
    hear in the winds
    the song of the anchor
    Her /stout/heart

9
at Te Weke Marae Te Poho o Tamatea's sacred voice rises like
high paddles over the rough music of waves calling the Antarctic
explorers back to the world of light welcoming them to first cast
anchor at Te Rāpaki-o-Te Rakiwhakaputa to pray and rest in the
strong arms of Whare Taonga the carved house
    call in the waka
    let the sisters light
    the spirit pathway
    Ōtamahua /Quail /Island

LINCOLN JAQUES

Singapore

On the British Airways
flight via Singapore
I would only eat cornflakes.
My mother complained.

And even those I threw up.
In the Telok Blangah District
in Singapore, my mother feared
the dark alleyways, the men who sat
smoking, the whites of their eyes,
knives glinting
under belts.

She feared everything in our new
country too. Her later husband
told us stories of his time in
Singapore during the war, how
he had to step over the rotting corpses
laying in the streets. And in Burma—

he still called it that—he saw a woman
washing her face
in the river, a
Bengali tiger sneaking
up behind as she
rinsed her linen,
unaware.
He'd stop at the details.

All I remember is rain.

JACKSON McCARTHY

The Father

It was afternoon and I was standing outside the house thinking about John Ashbery. The sun was setting and everything. Suddenly a boy appeared in front of me. I thought his legs were dirty and was about to scold him for them—*Boy, what are you doing walking around with dirty legs?*—yeah, good, something like that. But really they were just hairy. In this way he reminded me of me. *What do you think of Ralph Hotere?* he said. *I like his early work*, I said, counting on one hand the number of his paintings I'd actually seen. Mostly I'd seen his work in a book. A nice big one that said HOTERE on the front in block capital letters. I invited the boy inside for dinner. He accepted, but I could see the restlessness in his eyes. As he moved, I grew older. Late in the night—early morning, really; too early for birds—he went out onto the country road to his country truck: red, bright, like a birthday present. Fifty white swans asleep in the back. I got dressed for work. There was damp under the collar; a light tint of frost on the window. He didn't know I was watching. I didn't know what he planned to do with all those swans.

Der Rosenkavalier

How do you have such a nice car? I asked. *It's nicer than both my parents' cars put together.* At this point I had never heard little droplets of Strauss, little gemstones though they were, and I was happy. I still believed that the battle between man and nature was an ongoing one, one that we were winning in English classrooms all across the country. This was before they tried to cancel me; our children were not yet born. Unborn rascals, you can only avoid the sun for so long! Indeed, he came to talk to me one morning on Waiheke Island. He had been babbling for hours because he had been alive for billions of years, until he finally said: *Unlike my sister, the Moon—or was she my wife? These unimportant things you start to forget.* Then off the top of his head came a line of verse, dropped like a coin of the donation box: *The sky's a bedsheet of blue.* I looked up at the sky, down at my sheets: it was true. And with that, he extinguished himself, plunging the world into darkness. It was the end of the world, but still money tempted me.

ALEXANDRA FRASER

Love Was Not on the Programme

We went to see anger
a big crowd   everyone wanted to be there
anger is large   and loud   classic really
we got tickets late
but squeezed our way to the front
it was a stunning savage performance
everyone went home sad

We met with sorrow
it was a bright day that day
the clouds high   wispy   inaccessible
there was nothing to hold on to

We knelt on concrete
writing placards for later
thick crayon on corrugated card
    Down with the patriarchy
    Climate change is murder
    Die racist scum

Someone had dotted the i's
with love-hearts
but they vanished in the rushings of rage

We struggle
holding our banners high against
the prevailing wind

DANIELLE HEYHOE

Pursuit

Three days after Alba became a mother, her breasts became full and excruciating. *Dolly Parton-esque* was what her husband thought of them, and he was disappointed, too, that at that same time they became forbidden. But he was not angry about it. He explained to her that he was only marvelling at the irony of large, untouchable breasts. How cruel life could be, he had said, smiling. He brushed his teeth over the basin while watching Alba's reflection in the vanity, the cracked mirror slicing her body in two. If he had told Alba about the terrifyingly beautiful woman he believed her to be, she would probably have cried.

Alba was not in the least bit interested in her husband's thoughts of her. She was cupping her thickened breasts, allowing the hot shower to scorch them—a sensation so intense, it was only made possible by the hope of soothing the agony of her milk coming in. In truth, Alba admired the newfound ability her breasts possessed. They could sustain the life of her newborn! She had had them for years of course, properly since she was fifteen, but back then they had been empty and futile. And there had been all those years before that when they hadn't existed at all. The astonishment she now had for her own body was too conceited to share with anyone. Even her husband.

Alba turned the shower off and lightly dried herself beside him as he spat blue foam into the basin. She pulled on large black underwear, but not before pressing a thick pad between her legs. Finally, smiling at him, she blew a strand of brown hair away from her eyes.

I think I'll go to bed seeing as the baby is asleep, she told him. She was becoming a bit ruffled by the way he now looked at her: with reverence, as one to be feared.

The coffee her husband made the next morning had a transparent quality to it, which is to say it had no quality at all. Less satisfying than water. Alba wanted to spit her mouthful into the vast chrome sink but her husband was watching her with a long, sombre expression—the baby had been up most of the night. Instead, she satisfied her impulse by imagining herself spitting gallantly into the sink, as if to say she was worth more than mediocre coffee. Did she really believe that? She needed only remember the engorged breasts clinging tightly to her torso under the pinstripe nightshirt to know for sure. With her husband watching her, the visualisation of her daring splutter of coffee would have to be sufficient. If you believe in the potency of your perceived experience, then it must be real and true—isn't that correct?

When Mark noticed her return the full mug to the bench, he asked if everything was all right. Alba shrugged, which is to refuse an answer altogether, and he took it hard. He sat on the bar leaner beside her, nibbling his homemade sourdough, then removed the sleeping baby from her arms, enveloping him into his solid chest. He had advocated for that breakfast bar back when they renovated, enchanted by the notion of his future three or four children sitting opposite him each morning, staring back as their father made coffee for their mother. My feelings of love for you are immense, he told Alba.

Love has very little to do with how you feel and more to do with what you carry out, Alba told him. And when she said it she spoke with conviction, as though she was telling him that cake with icing is not a substitute for a nutritious meal (no matter how much he liked it), or that very few people enjoy their job one hundred per cent of the time—like these were facts, known by everyone except him. She would have liked to stand up then, move to the rattan settee, but her legs were heavy from lack of sleep.

When she didn't move from the stool, which he had anticipated, knowing his wife as well as he did, he became apprehensive about what might happen next. Alba clearly had no intention of speaking again. It terrified him, her inability to recognise love, a feeling so deep and wide that he believed she had never felt it at all—not for him, not for their child in his arms.

Mark took the baby to the nursery to change his nappy and onesie, which had streaks of yellow spreading down the legs. He turned to face Alba from the kitchen door, anticipating her affectionate gaze, but she was holding her phone up to her face, smiling into its screen. Your mother loves you, he had whispered. But also, he was thinking that it was impossible to engage with her without feeling afraid. Still, he would keep trying. His breath swirled between him and the baby—it held the faint whiff of excrement and he made a note to brush his teeth after he'd dressed the child.

In the afternoon, as he predicted, both Alba and the baby fell asleep on their queen-sized bed. He dressed quickly out of his flappy pyjama bottoms—the blue and white checks having unified over the years—and pulled on a pair of jeans. He had planned to tell Alba that he was going to the supermarket but she was still asleep. He'd read somewhere online that women needed additional sleep post childbirth, so after taking a deep inhale of the baby's forehead, which made his eyes water, he left them sleeping to find his car keys among piles of paper on the bench. Alba's coffee was still there, cream coagulating at its surface. He poured it out, rinsed the cup and left it upside down.

The traffic was sparse on the roads around their house. He stopped for one red light, counting the seconds until it turned green, *one, two, three, four, five, six* … It was easy to find a park right outside the library at two o'clock on a Wednesday. He was greeted by the nod of a woman just inside the door who smiled each time the scanner beeped the barcode of a book. She seemed to enjoy her job one hundred per cent of the time.

Silence rang throughout the large room when the beeps paused, and he felt he had to whisper right beside the woman's ear in order not to be overheard.

Do you have a section on motherhood?

He was trying not to be too breathy, having forgotten after all to brush his teeth.

The woman made a movement that looked pained, shuffling away from his face. She didn't say anything, but he followed her along the aisle to the back of the library where she pointed to some shelves.

Nobody spoke to him or even noticed him crouching down on the thin carpet, pulling out books, but then a woman about Alba's age was standing beside him. She stroked the spines on the top shelf of the motherhood section, stopping on a book titled *You're Good Enough*. He wasn't sure whether the title sent the right message—was one ever *good enough*? He thought of his own mother, finger curled through the Uniden phone cord, legs draped over the back of the couch when other mothers were feeding their children dinner.

He wondered whether his mother read this book back when he was a boy.

When the woman left the motherhood section, having taken no book for herself, he pulled *You're Good Enough* off the shelf and opened the initial pages. First published 1962. It was quite possible his mother had read it. He felt a deep sadness for his mother then, almost like a gesture of forgiveness. He quickly returned the book to the shelf. He kept smiling though. He would find a book that had space for Alba to fill.

I've found it! he told the librarian, having forgotten his previous resolve to remain unheard and unknown. The woman took the book and his library card from him, smiling when the scanner made a loud *beep*. She returned both to his grip without as much as a good day to you. Snooty little intellectual, he thought.

When Alba awoke, she startled into a sitting position. Quickly she felt around the duvet for the baby and found him unmoved, wrapped in muslin and still sleeping. His tiny breath came out of his nostrils in sudden milky puffs and her breasts felt pummelled from inside. She had a memory. Back when Mark had been pursuing her, he had invited her to his mother's house for cheese and an aperitif. They had sat on his mother's blue velvet sofa drinking Campari with vermouth on ice. It was bitter and without warmth. The conversation had been pleasant enough but the content had been courteous, almost distant. Mark and his mother had not hugged or kissed on the cheek when they arrived. A formal goodbye had been said upon departure and Alba did not see her again until their wedding day. Alba had been amazed by Mark's ability to overcome an unfeeling childhood—she had made love to him that afternoon for the first time.

Alba leaned her head back on the duvet now, thinking about lying beside him. She ached for her husband then, for the first time since before the baby. She could almost smell the scent of sleep and their aromatic sandalwood shower gel threaded through the hairs of his beard, pink lips poking through black fuzz. His body had always felt thick and immoveable when he lay beside her. She almost cried with longing for him. His small but intentional affections appeared in her mind like popping candy that she'd bought from the dairy as a child. Waiting for him lulled her back into a dreamlike state.

As she waited, the memories were overtaken by irritation. He had left no note, which was unlike him. She felt abandoned, charged with caring for the baby on her own when she was already sleep deprived.

When from the hallway she finally heard the turning of the lock, the stomping of boots on wooden floorboards, she simply cancelled out the fond memories. It was as though her afternoon of longing hadn't been real. And when Mark popped his head around the bedroom door and approached to kiss her, she rolled away from him, almost onto the sleeping child, recoiling from his musty breath.

You're still tired, he said. Go back to sleep until the baby needs feeding.

That evening, after what seemed like several hours of breastfeeding on the sofa while watching *The Bachelor*, Alba decided to put the baby down to sleep.

Mark said, You think he's ready for bed?

Alba had not said anything about the baby being ready for bed. She only knew that she was tired and hungry, and her nipples were sore. She scooped the little guy up into her arms and carried him to the bedroom still attached to her softening breast. She could still smell his milky newness. When she reached the bassinette at the end of their bed she pushed her pinkie finger into the corner of his suckling mouth to release the suction and swiftly placed him on the mattress. He screamed, his face scrunching up like discarded paper, and reeled around as though in pain. Alba closed the door and went to eat her dinner.

I have a book for you about motherhood, Mark said, once she was seated.

Alba took a bite, then looked away from the roast beef and grilled tomatoes on her plate. She chewed, then swallowed quickly and said: You have a book for me about motherhood?

The baby's wailing was continuous and blaring. It occurred to Mark that he may not have been easily heard above the child's roar. He nodded, smiling.

Alba placed the fork on her plate beside the sliced beast. Do you also have a book for yourself about fatherhood?

It was a very good question. He nodded, but it was insincere. He hadn't even thought to visit the section on fatherhood and the realisation came as a blow. No, I don't, but you have a good p—

Why do I need a book about motherhood?

Crying still sounded from the bedroom. Mark placed his knife and fork on the table and went to retrieve the baby. He returned with the child curled into his neck and the boy fell asleep to the rhythm of his chewing.

Why do I need a book about motherhood? Alba asked again.

Mark was surprised. They were both avid readers and he was aware—his wife had taught him—that there was always more to learn and understand. Only the week before Alba had gone into labour she'd arrived home from the mall with a coffee-table book titled *Sourdough, it's Not Playdough*, and he had been grateful that she recognised the importance of his hobby.

Alba stood up, her meal half eaten, and went to the bedroom. Mark sat quietly on his chair.

She couldn't recall later how long she spent in the bedroom watching the empty bassinet. Often, time was all the communication that was required. Her husband had always been a slight enigma to her. Mark had spoken about children from the moment she met him—which seemed incongruent, considering his mother. He took the opportunity almost every time they passed a child: look at that little boy in the playground, he's dropped his ice-cream; isn't it sweet how that girl smiles with her nose bunched up like that; the neighbours' kid could come to our place while he waits for his parents to get home, don't you think?

Alba had never thought about the boy at all, even when she saw him waiting on his front doorstep in the rain. She pitied her husband—how used up he was by the neediness of others. She remembered, then, all the times he had driven her home from college parties after she had spewed on their friends' parents' rugs, and how he hadn't tried anything on her. He'd cleaned her up, tucked her into the flannel bedsheets and left the dorm. Perhaps some people were just born with a greater capacity to think of others.

After a while, Alba heard a ripping sound from the dining room, followed by a resounding thunk on the wooden floorboards.

The baby must have fallen to the floor.

The baby must have fallen to the floor and was silent.

Alba lurched from the bed and swung the door open. The baby was indeed on the floor, but he was curled up on the sheepskin rug, his pink mouth open and wet. Sleeping. No sign of having been dropped at all.

However, metres from the baby lay the library book, torn in half.

When she thinks of this now, she always recalls a deep sense of urgency. In her memory the urgency is coming from her own voice. No! I *want* the book!

The book looked like two pieces of a puzzle that had been missing but were now found. She sees herself running across the floorboards and almost skidding to a halt on her knees. She sees herself look from the book to the baby, her breasts becoming rigid, filling with milk. All she had to do was look at the baby; her body knew what to do, her pale blue T-shirt turning navy around the nipples.

What she really did was walk around the dining table to the book and pick it up. She pressed together the two pieces of the book her husband had chosen for her at the library.

Mark was instantly filled with guilt. You don't need the book, he had told her, almost pleading. I'll pay for it at the library tomorrow, but you don't need it. I'm sorry.

He had been looking at the dark patches on her T-shirt.

Alba shook her head and said, I want the book. Do we have sellotape wide enough? Narrow sellotape would be too visible on the thick spine.

Mark went to his office and returned with a roll of tape. Pushing aside the plates and glasses, he motioned for Alba to sit beside him. She held the two sides of the book together as he pulled a long piece of tape from the roll and cut it off. Stretching it tightly, he covered the whole spine of the book and pummelled his fingertips over the tape until all air bubbles had escaped. His fingers brushed the tips of Alba's nails.

The baby started to stir, a moan escaping his small throat.

Alba laid the restored book on the wooden table. She smiled at it, then lightly rested her hand on her husband's forearm, making circles in the black curls with her fingertips.

BILL NELSON

Bird Life

A tūī finds itself
on the kitchen floor
at sunrise, a storm of heat,
claws curled, sleeping,
the house is cold,
a glass cabinet,
a bowl of crushed Weetbix.
I trap the cat inside,
watch her squirm
like the sunrise,
an internal mirror,
my small son
about to wake.
The tūī stirs, slams
into a window pane,
a shadow crosses
the surface of the sun
and the house darkens.
My son wakes, his tiny pips
of panic tumble down the stairs.
The bird that can't be caught
is now still, allows me to curl
my hand around its body.
As I release it outside, it lifts
for a moment toward the sun,
then tucks its wings and dives
into the dark undergrowth.

BRENT KININMONT

Near Things

The Levant, 1942

The horizon pencilled
behind the steamer;

a grey plume where
their island was.

A month of patrols.
Sulphur pools, too.

Not bathing now among
the bougainvillea.

His hot skin *no longer*
buttered on.

•

They pitched tents beside
an ancient quarry,

the camels idling there.
Beyond the humps:

the Giza Plateau.
That first night he flew

down the pyramid ramps
on sleds unloaded in his sleep.

The relief, he writes,
was immense.

•

Another packed carriage.
Shirtless the troopers

are riding the roof.
Through a sloping bend

they lumber.
A brown coin in hand

he reaches down,
plucks from the long branch

of the Bedouin's arm
a scorched melon.

•

Peggy, June, the two *Hildas*.
Names inscribed

in other shovels.
On the pass they are widening

he's already broken
two shafts.

That steel head he keeps
but won't christen.

*Only a fool would
get attached.*

•

Softly the leaves paw.
He's hiked all along

towards such affection,
but won't linger.

Barrelling off through the thicket:
a head eclipsed

by the rump.
From its side of the ridge

the bear hadn't heard
his boots till they crested.

•

The rope-tow isn't working.
To halfway they lug

the borrowed skis,
then race around him.

Grinning back and forth
across the slope

his novice tracks.
All those junctures in the snow.

Fleeting records
of *near things*.

ANYA SINCLAIR

Flowers

1. 433, 2022,   1370 x 1210mm
2. childhood, 2023, 1250 x 1180mm
3. 488, 2023, 1250 x 1100mm
4. flowers in landscape, 2023, 960 x 710mm
5. 461, 2023, 710 x 610mm
6. 491, 2023, 570 x 490mm
7. 317, 2022, 510 x 460mm
8. 173, 2022, 900 x 750mm

All acrylic on unstretched canvas.

PORTALS OF PRESENT TENSE

'I am inclined to believe that there is no such thing as repetition,' said Gertrude Stein. Instead of repetition, she argued for insistence, a concept that forms the basis for her infamous quote, 'a rose is a rose is a rose.' Sinclair's flowers provoke a kind of Steinian response in the viewer: a flower is a flower is a flower. Her works insist that we pay attention, through a lens of the temporal, the affective, the painting-as-doing. There is—to invoke Stein again—a continuous presence to these works. Sinclair draws our gaze into the notion of the verb—the making—in what she calls 'an antidote to the methodical.' The labour of these paintings is not in the curation or the framing; rather, Sinclair's flowers are existential, moment-driven, and offer, in her words, 'portals' into the present tense. The paint runs, the flowers ooze; the objects are electrified by their own materiality. As we too are electrified in our gazing, our doing-with the paintings, these portals of present tense.

—Lynley Edmeades

AHIMSA TIMOTEO BODHRÁN

Afloat (Our Daily Bread)

Back and forth, still rocking, womb returned I am, after hours on the water, how cradled we are, rocked, how we from one into another, lake paddle, loons loom, gulls grace our paths, intervening, ducks amuck, and here, mink sink, beavers darkly dome. Dragonflies, mid-flight, mate. Hover and redirect. Keel, kneel. An oar in my hands feels good. From one wet entry to another, stern wet bows tied, pulled too port, starboard slide, ashore, interlocate, alternate, invertebrate, we switch sides, face each other. Amphibian. Mine the water. Wood, I turn and churn again. Unexploded ordinances, let us, gentle giant, georelocate. Disarmed finally. Ballistics thwarted, yoked, batter buttered. Leading another man safely through these waters, ours, deeper into cyan unZioned, wet sons sunkiss without phosphorus burning. Guns wail. Being led from behind. Swimming in the wake of another vessel, his body through the water warmed for my passage. Underwater swim, I, but do not permanently submerge. Another day for pyres, nights ablaze. Until finally rest, we, aqua agitate. My feet, algae-blessed-held. Firm warm foundation for breezes to bless us. Dry salts. We talk about places hidden from hegemons, canoe-haul onto shore, knotted spots secreted, secreted into memory, stippled, stapled, how many I have loved, both lados ladders we climb and again, agile águilas grace our shoulders, we among pines, cactus always find ourselves, lapped by waves, newly breached, beached, manhandled, feathers floating in the water.

                        If you were here, and he, you, I'd lift your pungent pits into my mouth, take your tongue, clingstone now free, into mine, water-based, would elide into ellipses, rut like elk, new antlers emerging thorny from our horned flesh, shed velvets afloat, we would these waters bless, murky the depths, emerge with new scrapes and bruises, berries blue our skins, would bandage you, rub ointment, salve into your flesh saved, beso each boo-boo, offer mine for los labios, as we lick the lake, akin, again, from our fresh-washed flesh. Tattoo some new memory, matri-patrilined, of what we remember from before we were born. Some new place, intercoastal, for eagles to perch, each of us in each other's mouths, alas ascendant once more. Soaring, sonorous. Our breath in each other's ears, oars floating forever in each other's waters, churning. So do we each other's territories know, having paddled through them, time and again, place and amen. Sanctified in sweat, baptismed in blood, oh holy hosts we graciously greet; take into our mouths, diligently, daily, and swallow. Golondrinas.

AMBER FRENCH

bleak time

the canal was empty and snaking
not so firm as I remembered

small, I mean hand sized / secure and anonymous
disposal / but keeping some pale pink petals to cluster at the base of walls /
a dream I had / once / black hen black dog jumping / up / a fine / fine sifted
sand / a fine layer of talcum powder / somewhere /

I caught these words from the air with my web / red swaying

weeds / tall like people
with red leaves at their feet
making new green swaying light /

this fabric is so tender /
these cups so tender

this house with its face open to the sun
the sky is a big background
and there's nothing behind / or beyond / our house

PAULA KING

Mr Andrew King

Mr Andrew King built houses in Wellington. Story goes he had one eye. His great niece is not sure about her mountain. Her dad wanted to move. Her mum wanted to stay. She wants to live in a villa one day, a tent another, a tree house another, a modern showroom another. She says the villa would probably be white with charcoal and black trimmings. And the fence, white and wooden, perhaps picket, a splash of tag to break it up a bit. She wants the white wooden gate—heavy. One that swings both ways. She wants the shutter that you lift and drop. She wants the little gate that stands beside in support of the big gate. She wants the big gate that stands beside in support of the little gate. She wants the gate open. She wants the path that leads to the steps, to the verandah, to the large hallway door and the floor with the antique rug. She wants no lawn. She wants a lawn. She wants the big Bronze Sculpture. Native Bird. She suffers dreams. Outside the gate, on this sunny day, a man in a coat with wilderness hair pushes an empty supermarket trolley. She thinks there is a street named after Mr Andrew King in Wellington.

JONNY EDWARDS

Living and Company

Tony had an eye for interior design. You'd never guess from his ratty brown T-shirt and doomsday-prepper beard, but the furniture in his small slice of the Puriri Apartments sausage flat complex was very mid-century. The chromes and speckled whites were meticulously positioned. For consistency, the items were all one brand. Anko. Tony could only assume it was from one of those cold European countries where everyone rode bikes.

On that particular morning he gripped one of the side table's rounded wooden legs with his thumb and forefinger and easily moved it a couple of centimetres to the left. So sleek, so lightweight. So … Scandinavian. That was the word. It was now perfectly in line with the coffee table and the delicate geography of the room had been restored. He then sat on one of his charcoal modernist couches and played the first on his list of whichever once-a-day cellphone games were popular that month.

Tony was an expert shopper. To think, he had tastefully kitted out that place with new furniture on a forklift driver's wages. Side table: $47, coffee table: $112. He was on his second pastel blue toaster of the year for the everyday low price of $17. It was as though Tony knew a secret. That anyone could achieve minimalist style. That if you walked through the city centre to where the footpaths became more sporadic, and made some well-timed dashes onto roundabouts, you entered a world in which dinner plates were $1 each. That was a fraction of what those capitalists at the Salvation Army Family Store were asking for. They took free donations, gouged the public and used the proceeds to fill their vaults. No, Tony knew better.

Wide stupid eyes appeared glaring through the glass of his ranch slider. Ollie was ogling his set-up again. His wanting breaths fogged the glass. To the outsider the two would look very similar. But they both knew Ollie's shorts were a little bit older and his backpack a little bit cheaper. He was nice enough, but Tony suspected that Ollie's jealousy of his station in life could drive him to do something truly unhinged one day. As soon as he clocked

Tony's gaze, he scampered away.

Ollie lived two flats down. His came pre-furnished with couches that had likely been bought and sold many times in their history. The wood was thick and heavy, so it was not worth the strain of moving anything around. He was taunted every day as he walked to his place past white tabletops and matte-grey textured vases set up like a showroom. It looked how air conditioning felt. Ollie picked up odd jobs here and there, which did not allow him Tony's luxuries. Even an affordable chair set would still equate to a half-year of pork specials at the roast shop. He picked the skin around his thumbnail as he imagined making that sacrifice.

Ollie was snapped into consciousness by his own leg reflexively jerking forwards to stomp on a scuttling cockroach. These visitors were so regular that his muscles had perfected the motion to the point where he only noticed after the bugs were squashed. This always made him feel smug. He heard somewhere that cockroaches could endure a nuclear blast, yet they couldn't survive his right boot.

Ollie's place wasn't a hovel or anything. There were dirtier, more worn-down flats on Puriri Street. It was just that bugs seemed to thrive in the mugginess that lingered for most of the year. And sure, he probably didn't wipe spilled spots of jam from his tabletops as thoroughly as some people who had more reason to be house proud.

Along with cockroaches were the swarms of flies. Ollie had a strategy for fly swatting, for which he used the free weekly community newspaper, rolled and folded. Ollie once read an article on his fly swat about a local possum eradication project and how it was very important now that 80% of the possums had been killed that they got the other 20%. This was because the surviving 20% were the possums that were good at not getting caught in traps and if they were left to reproduce you would have the same number of possums as before, but they'd all be good at not getting caught in traps. For this reason, he wouldn't go for the easy, big doddering targets that remained on the glass even when his execution device was in striking distance. Instead, Ollie stalked, sometimes for 20 minutes each, the most zippy and irritating little flies in the hopes of creating a placid and harmless population.

Once the corpses littered the floor, Ollie would gather a handful and take it to one of his whitetail webs. (The residents of Puriri Street referred to most spiders as whitetails, because they could always find white traces on them. Their beliefs were reinforced by nasty infections they regularly developed on their bodies. Dr Manson was more sceptical, noting the number of 'spider bites' that arrived in her clinic was far out of proportion to the estimated number of venomous spiders in the area.) Ollie would flick a fly into the web and tap it to alert the spider. When one appeared and began wrapping its food, Ollie would throw in another. Sometimes he scattered several at once to keep the spider occupied. He continued this game for as long as he could sustain the spider's interest. When it left his company after becoming full, bored or confused, Ollie often didn't know what to do with himself.

He heard the clanging of bottles. It was Tony taking out his glass recycling. He couldn't resist the chance of a conversation. Ollie grabbed the third-full bin from his kitchen floor and rushed outside.

'Hey Tony. Geez, that crash out on the coast yesterday. Horrible stuff, huh?'

Ollie didn't care so much about the content of conversations, nor did he really listen to the answers. What he liked was being part of making chatter. Like his flies into the spider web, he threw out non-sequitur questions in various directions, often before the last one had been fully answered.

'How were the snapper at the weekend?'

'Ugh, do you reckon this heat is going to last?'

'Beaut new side table. Where'd you get it?'

He made the fatal error of feeding Tony a question that could be wrapped up with one word. Tony quickly followed this with an 'I'll let you get back to it' before Ollie could recuperate. Tony wanted to go inside to get his toast, but that would mean walking past Ollie and risking further conversation. Instead, he paced on to the street. Besides, he had a mission today.

Puriri Street was made up of blocks of flats, broken up by quaint old villas maintained by quaint old ladies. The street lay in a town that by New Zealand standards was considered a city. As Tony strode down the street, the fragrance of frangipanis was overtaken by the smell of Original Recipe. His destination was beyond town, to the imposing warehouses in the distance that sold lemon trees, pencil sharpeners and salad bowls. Each store you could recognise by its trademarked colour from as far as the peninsula lookout.

There were a few holdouts in the city centre though. Tony walked past Le

Cafe De Paris, which sold the best sausage rolls and custard squares in the region. Its interior walls were adorned with canvas block prints of the Eiffel Tower in various styles and from several angles and distances. It had black-and-white chequered lino floors, an office-style water cooler and decorative crates stacked against the walls. French tourists once came in asking for savoury crepes and received blank stares from staff. They settled for white bread egg sandwiches, which the owner Ruth argued contained many of the same ingredients, just in a different formation. A steady stream of regulars was enough to keep the business afloat so far, but Ruth was always tricked into thinking more customers were about to enter when she saw men peeking through the window. The reality was they had just come from the barber which recently opened next door. The clients, who thought it effeminate to care about the quality of their cuts or even acknowledge any difference while sitting in the chair, were sneaking glances of their side fades in Le Cafe De Paris' windows. Ruth wished a few more of the tables were filled with people she could have hard-case yarns with. She didn't even really mind if they bought anything. Some parents could just get their kids fluffies and Ruth could entertain them with her banter, which was a safe level of outrageous.

Tony kept walking until he saw a gloomy-eyed Joe changing the sign at the entrance to Joe's Palace. The imposing building, with its faded-green patterned carpet, was somewhere between a $2 shop and a department store. Everything that fell under the umbrella of bits and pieces spilled out of its shelves. It still clung on to the market for craft supplies, costumes and national flags. In its entire 42 years of operation, the shop's central advertising campaign had revolved around Joe's *crazy* prices. It was a dark open secret that at any given time the craziness of the prices, either high or low, was directly linked to the store owner's mental state. When Joe accidentally reversed his ute over his neighbour's cat Panda, frying pans were selling for $9 the next day. Once, on her way to work, Manaia the librarian called Joe's wife Maggie in a panic. Fairy tiaras were going for $2.83 each. She knew the specificity and unevenness in the cent column couldn't be good. It turned out Maggie was going to stay with her parents for a while to get some perspective on their relationship. This was why Joe's customers were relieved when prices were consistent with market rates. Joe gave Tony a solemn nod and walked back in the store. PVA glue $22 a bottle. Poor bastard.

Tony paced past the Sallies, but still managed to catch a sign for white bowls at $4 each in the window. Think of how many people had touched them with their grubby mitts. Tony thought about all the exploitation in the world and wondered how some people justified their actions.

He was now on the outskirts. The road continued, but the footpath gave way to gravel and then nothing. He hugged a bridge railing and then tightrope walked on the sliver of chip seal between the outer white line of the road and a ditch. Then, there they were. Majestic buildings that stood as the real equalisers in society. After a lurching dance through the car park, he reached the automatic doors of his preferred store.

The inside was vast and easily replicable. It would be easy for most to lose their way, but Tony was a veteran. Past the reduced-to-clear Halloween lollies and left at the off-brand board games with names like Property Investor! and Peckish Peckish Ponies. Soon he reached his lamp. Marble-based with an elegant thin black stem curving over into one of those big old barn lightbulbs that rich people had at weddings. Tony picked up one of the boxes, heaved it over his shoulder and took it to the self-checkout. After paying he thanked the employee, who was staring blankly into the store's clinical ceiling lights. He left and started his walk home, thinking about where the lamp could add the most atmosphere.

Tony sped up when he saw black smoke pluming from his street. As he got closer, he saw two fire engines parked outside the Puriri Apartments. He reached his flat, but couldn't see inside through the thick layers of black and grey. It smelled of damp ash. The firefighter said it was under control, but that his place wouldn't be liveable for a long time and suggested he found a friend to stay with. Tony didn't hear any of it. He was staring through the fireman's face thinking how cruel it was that so much beauty had been destroyed. Ollie peered out past his ranch slider, but whipped his head back inside once he saw Tony.

★

A few nights later, with nowhere else to go, Tony was sitting on Ollie's couch. He was still mourning. Although he had to admit, despite the different skin cells and human oils that thing must have collected over the years, the way you sunk into the cushion was pretty comfy.

It turned out that Tony's toaster had sparked and caused his faux-rattan mail basket to light. Someone promptly called the brigade after his alarm went off. But even with a seven-minute response time, his furniture had been wiped clean out by the time the crew arrived. The firefighters excitedly told their respective loved ones how they'd never seen anything burn so quickly. Through hunch rather than evidence, Tony still thought Ollie could be somehow responsible.

Ollie had sensed Tony's reluctance to talk was even greater than normal during his stay so far.

'You know, I did try and help. I was over at yours as soon as I heard the alarm.'

Tony ignored him.

Ollie went out outside and riffled through his bin bag. He came back in holding a fire extinguisher.

'Your door was open. I found this inside and tried to put it out.'

The fire extinguisher still had its pin in, but the handle had partially snapped and was limply hanging from the top of the tank. In stylish lower-case font at the bottom of the label it said 'anko'.

Tony processed this information.

'Thanks.'

He started playing a word game on his phone. Today's was particularly hard. Quite consonant heavy. Tony thought about how it was actually quite comforting to have someone around to ignore.

'Geez, what do you think about that protest out at the refinery?' Ollie asked.

'Sorry mate, I'm just trying to concentrate here.'

The Landfall Review

Landfall Review Online

www.landfallreview.com
Reviews posted since October 2022
(reviewer's name in brackets)

October 2022

Jumping Sundays: The rise and fall of the counterculture in Aotearoa New Zealand by Nick Bollinger (Philip Matthews)
Butcherbird by Cassie Hart (Gina Cole)
Next: Poems 2016–2021 by Alan Roddick (Harry Ricketts)
Night School by Michael Steven (Harry Ricketts)
Sonnets for Sio by Scott Hamilton (Harry Ricketts)
The Other Way by David Trubridge (Erik Kennedy)
Beats of the Pa'u by Maria Samuela (Iona Winter)
Peninsula by Sharron Came (Iona Winter)

November 2022

Seasons by William Direen (Robyn Maree Pickens)
Resonating Distances by Richard von Sturmer (Robyn Maree Pickens)
Breach by Lisa Samuels (Robyn Maree Pickens)
Na Viro by Gina Cole (Sally Blundell)
Anzac Nations: The legacy of Gallipoli in New Zealand and Australia 1965–2015 by Rowan Light (Robert McLean)
Slow Down, You're Here by Brannavan Gnanalingam (Chris Else)
The Stupefying by Nick Ascroft (Victor Billot)
Gorse Poems by Chris Holdaway (Victor Billot)

December 2022

Notes on Womanhood by Sarah Jane Barnett (Wendy Parkins)
You Probably Think This Song is About You by Kate Camp (Wendy Parkins)
No Other Place to Stand: An anthology of climate change poetry from Aotearoa New Zealand edited by Jordan Hamel, Rebecca Hawkes, Erik Kennedy and Essa Ranapiri (Francis Cooke)
A Book of Rongo and Te Rangahau by Briar Wood (Arihia Latham)
Sedition by Anahera Gildea (Arihia Latham)
Gaylene's Take: Her life in New Zealand film by Gaylene Preston (Mary Macpherson)
droplet by Sheryl Campbell (Mary Macpherson)
Return to Harikoa Bay by Owen Marshall (Philip Temple)
On Elephant's Shoulders by Sudha Rao (Vaughan Rapatahana)
Expectation by Tom Weston (Vaughan Rapatahana)
Echidna by essa may ranapiri (Vaughan Rapatahana)
By the Green of the Spring by Paddy Richardson (Catherine Robertson)
Mrs Jewell and the Wreck of the General Grant by Cristina Sanders (Catherine Robertson)
Everyone is Everyone Except You by Jordan Hamel (Airini Beautrais)
A Question Bigger than a Hawk by Jan FitzGerald (Airini Beautrais)
People Person by Joanna Cho (Airini Beautrais)
Thief, Convict, Pirate, Wife: The many histories of Charlotte Badger by Jennifer Ashton (Sarah Christie)

February 2023

Unseasoned Campaigner by Janet Newman (Vincent O'Sullivan)
What Fire by Alice Miller (Vincent O'Sullivan)
A Riderless Horse by Tim Upperton (Erik Kennedy)
Surrender by Michaela Keeble (Erik Kennedy)
Naming the Beasts by Elizabeth Morton (Erik Kennedy)
Toi Tū Toi Ora: Contemporary Māori art edited by Nigel Borell (David Eggleton)
To Be Fair: Confessions of a District Court Judge by Rosemary Riddell (Helen White)

March 2023

Drinking With Li Bai by Doc Drumheller (Michael Steven)
Surprised by Hope by John Gibb (Michael Steven)
Sheep Truck by Peter Olds (Michael Steven)
Sign Language for the Death of Reason by Linda Collins (Shana Chandra)
Island Notes: Finding my place on Aotea Great Barrier Island by Tim Higham (Shana Chandra)
Small Bodies of Water by Nina Mingya Powles (Shana Chandra)
The Song of Globule: 80 sonnets by Stephen Oliver (Patricia Prime)
Heroides: 15 sonnets by Stephen Oliver (Patricia Prime)
Te Motunui Epa by Rachel Buchanan (Andrew Paul Wood)
The Frog Prince by James Norcliffe (Jack Ross)
Culture in a Small Country: The arts in New Zealand by Roger Horrocks (David Eggleton)
A Book of Seeing by Roger Horrocks (David Eggleton)

Quardle oodle ardle wardle doodle
Chris Else

The Axeman's Carnival by Catherine Chidgey (Te Herenga Waka University Press, 2022), 350pp, $35

One of the novels I most enjoyed last year and certainly my favourite New Zealand novel was Bryan Walpert's *Entanglement*. My pick so far this year is *The Axeman's Carnival* by Catherine Chidgey. I would not be surprised if it was still my pick at the end of the year.

I mention these two books in the same breath because they share several characteristics. Both are notable for their intelligence and their subtlety. Both use ideas not in the service of a didactic purpose but as literary devices on a par with metaphor. Both apply their intellectual content to the exploration of small domestic stories of relationships under stress and thereby lift those relationships out of the ordinary.

They are differences too, of course. Walpert's ideational framework is tightly controlled and scientific, drawn from the study of time, and the drama of his story is rendered all the more fateful and heart-rending by the logic that reveals it. In Chidgey's case, despite the violence at the story's core, the effect is comic and satirical and the framework is literary. The novel is full of tropes, some of them specific to New Zealand literature, that are glanced at or pushed to their limits or turned upside down. One way to read this playful and witty book is as a grand spoof of the Great New Zealand Novel.

The story centres on Rob and Marnie, a couple in their thirties struggling to make a go of a high-country sheep farm. Rob is handsome, hard working and a first-class axeman. He has won the Golden Axe at the annual carnival nine years in a row and, despite fierce competition from a new young rival, Ethan bloody McKay, is determined to make it ten.

Rob and Marnie love each other, and Rob is considerate and kind except when he's had a bellyful and his jealousy and fury break free. Chidgey's portrayal of the violence is matter-of-fact in the manner of much local modern fiction, leaving the reader to react to the horror of it. Rob's abject apologies after the event sound sincere and Marnie's loyalty to the relationship, which leads her to hide her bruises under makeup and long-sleeved blouses, seems born of stoicism rather than fear.

In one sense, Marnie holds the upper hand and knows it. One of Rob's beatings has led to a miscarriage and, in an echo of one of Chidgey's earlier novels, *The Wish Child*, the ghost of the dead baby casts a shadow over the story. The miscarriage is never spoken of openly but nor is Rob ever allowed to forget it. The moral high ground gives Marnie a degree of freedom, which she exploits judiciously. One of her projects, in the face of Rob's derision, is to rescue and hand-rear a nestling magpie fallen from a nest in a stand of pines on the farm.

So far, so familiar. The tough life of the high-country farmer in an endless struggle against an inhospitable landscape is a well-established trope in Pākehā culture; so too is the drunken husband beating up his wife. There must be dozens of stories and novels, many of the latter self-published, that trace these themes from early colonial times to the present day. What lifts *The Axeman's Carnival* out of the ordinary, apart from the exceptional skill of its author, is Chidgey's choice of the magpie as narrator. Given that the bird is a surrogate for Marnie's lost baby, there is another faint echo of *The Wish Child* here.

In Denis Glover's iconic poem the magpies provide a mocking chorus to the efforts of the young couple struggling to make a go of their farm:

> Year in year out they worked
> While the pines grew overhead,
> And *Quardle oodle ardle wardle doodle*
> The magpies said.

Ultimately it is the unforgiving landscape, which the birds represent, that wins. From this notion Chidgey elaborates a thematic network in which the mockery reaches into every aspect of the story.

Marnie names the magpie Tama. This, as one of the characters observes, has a Māori ring to it—tama in te reo means son, boy or nephew, and the territorial disputes between the birds up in their pines and the humans on the ground around them might be read as a correlate for colonialism. The magpies seem tribal in their organisation, and Tama's father speaks with the mana of a warrior demanding utu. Chidgey is too smart to leave this as any more than a suggestion, however. The magpie is, after all, an Australian species introduced by nineteenth-century colonists and, in any case, Tama is also short for Tamagotchi, the Japanese digital pets that were a global fad in the late 1990s.

Such ambiguity extends to the character of Tama himself. He is both bird and human. Chidgey draws on the characteristics of his species, but her purpose is not to explore the natural life of another creature in the way, for example, that Philip Temple explores the world of the kea in his novel *Beak of the Moon*. Instead, she fashions a hybrid being who inveigles his way into Marnie and Rob's life and turns it upside down. Although he ultimately redeems himself in his father's eyes, his choice, ultimately, is to stay in the human world rather than return to the pines.

Tama is a tireless and astute observer of the goings-on around him. He takes in the workings of the farm; the interactions and conversations between Marnie and Rob and their extended family; and even the stereotyped plots and dialogue of their favourite TV programmes. Now and again his natural talent for mimicry leads him to reproduce sounds he has heard, including snatches of speech. These random utterances make him the master of the non sequitur. Here, for example, is a passage in which Marnie and Rob are discussing the rats that have invaded the ceiling of their decaying house:

> In the roof something scuttled and scuffed. Something skittered and thumped.
> Marnie said, 'It sounds like they are going to crash right through. Land in our laps.'
> 'I'll get the poison myself,' said Rob. 'A broad spectrum one, eh, Tama?' He nudged me with the poker. 'Yum yum yum.'
> 'Yum yum yum,' I said.
> He stood the fire guard in front of the fire, and then he turned on the TV to watch his crime show about young lovers stumbling across the corpse of a beautiful unclothed woman in the park. *One partial print on the barrel. Run it through the database, Trent.*
> 'They deal with this kind of thing all the time,' said Marnie. 'We need professional help.'
> 'You just have to know how to think like a rat,' said Rob, levering up the footrest on his TV chair.
> 'She's been dead for at least twelve hours,' I said.
> Marnie held her hands out to the heat. 'They can start fires, you know. Chew through electric cables.'
> 'Those are defensive wounds,' I said.
> 'I'll do it myself,' said Rob. 'Save some money for a change.'
> Rustle, scuttle, scuffle, thud.

Such passages operate on three levels. First there is the interaction between the human characters who ignore the bird for much of the time. Then there are the affectless observations and utterances of Tama himself. Finally, there is the reaction of the reader who can't help but take his random remarks as oblique commentary on what the humans are up to. This interplay is the source of much of the book's wit.

As the story moves forward, Tama's role changes from observer and adjunct to an active participant in the story and Rob's rival for Marnie's affections. Her projection of her frustrated maternal feelings leads to her dressing him up in dolls' clothes and taking photos and videos. She begins posting these on Instagram, and they quickly develop a following that snowballs.

She and Rob hire a social media expert who helps monetise Tama's fame through merchandising and advertising. The returns are impressive enough to offer the prospect of a debt-free farm. Rob, who has always viewed Tama with scarcely veiled hostility, buries his jealousy beneath a phoney enthusiasm for the subject of his new-found fortune.

In private, though, the marriage is under increased pressure. Events at the Axeman's Carnival lead to a violent outburst in which the whole edifice comes crashing down. At this point Tama intervenes in the manner of an archetypal hero and rescues the heroine, first by exposing Rob's duplicity and then by delivering the ultimate comeuppence. The story ends with hero and heroine on the brink a happy-ever-after, although the romance is undermined by an ironic echo of *The Two Ronnies*:

> In the master bedroom Marnie lifted the cushions from the master bed: the cushion with the sheepswool sheep and the cushion with the dead lavender and all the satiny

heartshaped cushions. Then she folded back the blankets and climbed in, and I climbed in too. The rain began to patter on the roof.
  'Goodnight, Tama,' she said.
  'Goodnight, Tama,' I said.
  And then we slept.

Thus the magpies triumph once again.
  I thoroughly enjoyed this subtle, witty and smartly ironic book, although I did wonder if Chidgey was piling it on thick in order to rid herself of the burden of writing another Kiwi story. I hope not.

Less Pristine Snow
Jenny Powell

Winter Time by Laurence Fearnley (Penguin Random House, 2022), 304pp, $36

The Mackenzie Country, close to the central spine of the South Island Te Waipounamu, is a tourist mecca in the summer, but low temperatures in winter can limit access and activities. Picturesque frosts are accompanied by treacherous conditions. Accidents happen. Hoar frosts attach breath-taking crystalline chandeliers to solid objects, but the rapid onset of the heavier rime ice and its claustrophobic fog brings potential dangers. This wonderland panorama enclosing the Mackenzie Country forms the background to Laurence Fearnley's most recent novel, *Winter Time*. It also becomes the foreground.

  In Fearnley's Mackenzie heartland, hills and mountains, along with a glacier-fed lake, surround the fictional village of Matariki. Winter, with its harsh conditions, sets the daily timetable for village residents in the season, dominating their lives, including that of recent arrival Roland March. Following the death of a younger brother, Roland has travelled from his voguish Sydney apartment to attend to the empty family home in Matariki, where a deep midwinter chill permeates the house.

  Fearnley explains in her Author's Note

that the sense of touch is a prime focus in *Winter Time*. Tactility is present from the first sentence: 'Roland stood in the middle of the road, his brother's mountain bike propped against his thigh, the weight of it comforting.'

The explanation of Roland's circumstances and his family's backstory is so confidently constructed in the prologue that there is a slight sense of jarring in moving from that deft compression to the stylistic flow of the main text, with its subtle emphasis on uncertainty and oppressiveness.

In fact, holding his brother's bike, a faint sense of discomfort nags at Roland as he takes in his old home town. He cycles to the location of his brother's accident. Debris indicates where Eddie's Hilux left the road, toppled down the bank and plunged into the canal. While water opened and shut over Eddie stuck inside the ute, it was not, as Roland realises, an open and shut case.

Tragically, Roland is the only family member left who can investigate the hidden chain of prior events. His parents are dead and, in a cruel domino effect, all of his siblings have now died of various causes. Born and raised in Matariki, Roland dutifully stayed on following the departure of his father and death of his mother, until his younger sister and two brothers had left school. The younger siblings honed skilful interactions with their environment growing up, but Roland's sensitivity prevented his similar participation. His father labelled him as 'soft'.

In Roland, Fearnley creates a perennial outsider. He should at least be a partial member of Matariki's inner group, but he is inescapably different. In Sydney he lives with his gay partner and together they run Kernel, a wholefoods shop. But to satisfy himself about the nature of Eddie's death, Roland must gain at least some knowledge of village dynamics and politics.

Winter Time adroitly instigates conflict. Subtly skated over or overtly ice-cracking, characters and environments converge. Roland has retained his geographical memory of the wider Matariki area. His experience and observations stem from Fearnley's own, and, as an artist sensitively builds up layers of paint to evoke depth and detail, so Fearnley builds her narrative phrase by phrase:

> The closer he got to the lake, the less pristine the snow was. Tracks from numerous vehicles cut up the cover, turning it into a mushy, muddy yellow. In the distance, however, the hills around the lake appeared cast in various tones of blue. From the water through to the pale silver blue of the slopes and then the bands of bright blue sky, the landscape struck him as being timeless, or, rather, outside of time, existing beyond the world of ordinary humans.

Currently, wherever he is, life seems to be unravelling for Roland. Both the Sydney shop and his partner are moving away from his personal values, and at Matariki tension increases as he gathers information about Eddie's death. Additionally, Roland becomes trapped in an avalanche of social media posts in which he seemingly blames local groups for contributing to his brother's death. The problem is, he didn't write them.

He lacks the competence and confidence to confront his crumbling world. Yet, he is capable of profound realisations:

> It hit Roland with force that there was no one left in his family, no one who could nod with agreement and smile with recognition when he spoke about his growing years. Part of his life would now slowly, but surely, be erased from his memory. It unnerved him, the intensity of his single-ness.

Perhaps this is why Roland attaches himself to others, forming unlikely alliances. In her convincing portrayal of Roland's traumatised personality, Fearnley utilises these unexpected relationships as a diversion for Roland, away from his increasing desperation. They are also pivotal in adding to the mysteries of Matariki.

It is not only the presence of touch that is a focus in the novel, but the absence of touch, and the symbolism of that. As a child in Matariki during the onslaught of winter, Roland rubbed his toes until the rigid numbness of his foot slowly gave way to a stinging pain. Eddie would be kicking the chair in front of him, trying to pound some feeling back into his foot. The move from absence of feeling to presence is repeatedly bridged by physical or psychological pain.

Roland imagines Eddie's ute descending into the depths of the lake, with Eddie, perhaps rattling the door handle, hammering at the windscreen, kicking against the passenger windows, until the force of bubbles flowing from his mouth dwindles to nothing. Presence, pain and absence.

This imagining of Eddie's last frenzied efforts highlights the strong visual element of Fearnley's writing. As readers, we have to visualise the presence or absence of touch, while the novelist's use of the tropes of synaesthesia skilfully acknowledges an intertwining of the senses of sight and touch. The judicious employment of a palette of colours, too, is an important device for this writer. The all-enveloping winteriness, with the suggestive emptiness of the colour white, triggers a major loss of Roland's sense of location. As a precursor to this, Roland recalls his Sydney apartment with its stark white interior design. It was disorienting and he remembers how he longed to break up the monotonous house-scape with just a hint of colour.

Thus, unintentionally caught in a Matariki winter white-out, Roland attempts to cycle on to the next sighting of a house. His body, warm from the effort of biking, cools rapidly and eventually hypothermia threatens. He finds himself in a place without horizon, or measure of distance. Fog and snow create an absence of visual and tactile clues. Without vision, he has no reference point for movement, no sense of proprioception—of where his body is located in time and space.

> Covered in white powder, he crawled to his feet and looked around, unable to ascertain where he was, or what, exactly, he

was standing on. It could have been flat or the edge of a cliff; he didn't know, and his breathing again came rapidly and he had to speak into the void to make anything seem real.

This powerful merging of an external and internal white-out mirrors the magnitude of Roland's fragility. Though to feel lost is, in an insightful way, to be present, and Roland is highly capable of personal insights. He is ensconced in the thematic refrain of absence, pain and presence. Over time, some of his questions arrive on a path to answers while others remain in a fog of uncertainty. This is not too surprising. *Winter Time* is a novel making much of life's underlying connections which, after all, are not always recognised or resolved.

The cover blurb notes that Fearnley occupies a position somewhere between national treasure and experimental writer. There is no need for separate categories. For Fearnley, national treasure and experimental writer belong on the same signpost, pointing in the direction of truly memorable writing.

Nevertheless, She Persisted
Sally Blundell

Making Space: A history of New Zealand women in architecture, edited by Elizabeth Cox (Massey University Press, 2022), 448pp, $65

Architecture books arrive with certain expectations. Large, sleek, hardback expectations. Glossy images of dramatic interiors and disappearing glass frontages overlooking a secluded bay or amber-lit urban street; sentences that drift in arcs of lyricism. *Making Space* is not that sort of book. The pages are matt, the photos are mainly small and most are headshots. The text—and there is a truckload of text in this publication—is informative, important and straight to the point.

It begins with a rustle of skirts and the scratch of pencil on paper. In 1846 Marianne Reay, the wife of a clergyman, designs a small neo-Gothic timber church in Wakefield near Nelson. When finished, writes the local paper, it promises to be 'one of the most ornamental constructions in the settlement'. Three years later, sisters Mary and Ellen Taylor design a drapery shop and home in Cuba Street, Wellington. 'Our new house [de]lights us with its roomy comfort,' Mary wrote to her good friend Charlotte Brontë.

In 1913 Lucy Greenish becomes the first woman registered with the newly formed New Zealand Institute of Architects (NZIA) and the first woman to establish her own practice. There is no record of her work (plans at that time were often unsigned) and it is not known how long her practice lasted—in a street directory in 1930 she is listed as a gardener.

But it is Greenish, pictured leaning over a drawing board in long skirt, shirt and tie in the book's introduction, who inspired this book. Wellington historian Elizabeth Cox came across her name in a book on Wellington architects between 1840 and 1940. To Cox's surprise, Greenish was the only woman mentioned.

Unconvinced, Cox went to work, rummaging through family histories, newspaper articles, university records and NZIA archives to unearth evidence of 'dozens of women' working in architecture firms in the first half of the 20th century. 'Although I am a women's historian,' she writes, 'and know how easy it is for women to be forgotten, it was still surprising to discover afresh how easy it is for women to slip from view in the profession.'

Some could never have afforded the required tuition—under the early training system, students had to pay to be apprenticed to a senior architect. Some went on to work in architectural firms as draughtswomen but never registered as architects. Some, like the clearly talented Alison Shepherd, left to study overseas and never came back. Some were diverted down the more acceptable pathway of home decoration and 'interior beautification'; some abandoned their architectural aspirations the day they married. Many more, argues Cox, shaped our built environment with no acknowledgement or record.

In the 48 short, roughly chronological chapters that make up *Making Space*—its title points to the literal job of making spaces and the story of women architects making space for themselves within a male-dominated profession—Cox and 29 other academics, historians and architects direct our attention to those women who did persevere as draughtswomen, architects, architecture tutors, planners and landscape architects. The result, as Cox explains in her introduction, is more than a simple record showing 'she was here'. Like Barbara Brookes' *A History of New Zealand Women*, the book's strength lies in its many conversations about how women working in a male-dominated profession used their skills to bring about social change.

When Florence Field designed a house for her father, the mayor of Nelson, in the early 1920s, for example, she insisted on a modern, accessible, easy-to-clean kitchen aimed at reducing the drudgery of housework. When Kingitanga leader Te Puea Hērangi directed the construction of the new Tūrangawaewae marae, she also commissioned the carving of a new whare whakairo as a meeting house and hospital for her people.

When Mereana Tōpia decided to build a whare whakairo near Dargaville, her daughter Jane took up the challenge of carving. Despite the assumed gender division in the world of Māori carving, writes Tryphena Cracknell, 'Women have carved, women carve.'

Working within the Ministry of Works and other government departments, women architects responded to calls for social housing that was light, warm and well ventilated.

Since then, women have taken lead roles in large civic projects, including the NEW Gallery for Auckland Art Gallery Toi o Tāmaki (Julie Stout), Pātaka Art + Museum in Porirua (Anne Salmond) and Remuera Library (Lynda Simmons). As librarian and editor Catherine Hammond writes, 'It is now almost a given that a major civic project will include female representation or leadership.'

It has not been an easy road. Originally, Cox tells us, the subtitle of this book was going to be 'Nevertheless, she persisted'. The subtitle could have stayed—these are stories of extraordinary persistence.

Even as the number of women studying architecture grew—in 1976 a third of students were women—former graduates describe a learning environment that was, as architectural historian Julia Gatley has noted, 'distinctly male and masculine, if not chauvinistic'. Women high performers at architecture school were seen as 'wanna-bes and try-hards', says another, 'while the boys were seen as "the ones to watch".'

In the workforce, interviewees describe the experience of being the only female in a group of all-male architects, of being mistaken for the note-taker or coffee-maker at meetings, of being rejected by major clients on the basis of gender, of being overlooked for promotion during childbearing years, of having to fight for construction site experience, of exclusions from events, of physical and verbal harassment and put-downs.

They persisted, forming alliances, networks, women's groups, home offices, practices based around the needs of childcare; increasingly their voices were heard. Through events such as the *Constructive Agenda: 60 Years of Women in Architecture in New Zealand* exhibition in 1993 and new entities such as the national Māori women's carving group, Te Roopu o Ngā Wahine Kai Whakairo, the Architectural Centre in Wellington, the Group in Auckland, the Women's Institute of Architecture (later Women in Architecture), Architecture+Women NZ and Urban Auckland, women pushed for new approaches to housing, planning, education and work.

Elizabeth Aitken Rose's compelling profile on the pioneering Nancy Northcroft, co-founder of the New Zealand Planning Institute, reveals Northcroft's legacy in promoting new social objectives through town planning, architecture and education. Jessica Halliday documents the role of women as architects, landscape architects, Māori leaders and urban regeneration activists in the rebuild of Christchurch after the 2010–11 earthquakes.

In an excellent short essay, Ekta Nathu explains how women positioned themselves at the margins of architecture, where it commonly overlaps with 'socially progressive agendas' such as sustainable architecture, feminist practices and social housing. Just as early women architects used their skills to end kitchen drudgery, these new forms of activism within architecture have been applied to environmental sustainability (such as Wellington's award-winning First Light Studio) and housing reform (such as Earthsong, New Zealand's first purpose-built co-housing development). Similarly, the adoption of Te Aranga Principles, created in 2007 by Ngā Aho to incorporate Māori values in the design of new developments, indicates the ongoing challenge to better reflect tangata whenua through the built environment—as Whāngarei architect Jade Kaka asks, 'Why are people who are graduating in Aotearoa, who are going to become architects in Aotearoa, not being taught about the context, the architectural context, of this place?'

Some interviewees—and many of these contributions are styled as oral history projects—disliked the term 'women architects', preferring simply 'architects'. Cox insists that women architects do bring something different to a building, urban environment or landscape, 'and the body of evidence in this book goes some way to explaining just what this is'.

By this, she presumably means the ways in which women have used their own experiences and insight to improve the lives of those who live or work in these buildings. But it also suggests a recognition of the potential of architecture to better reflect, and respond to, the specific and diverse needs of Aotearoa New Zealand. As Simmons writes, the institutional acceptance of marginal communities within the broader architectural community 'can be seen as a sign that the activism of many decades has been, and continues to be, effective'.

Still, there are challenges.

While the proportion of women architecture graduates has grown, from 32 per cent in 2000 to just over half in 2018, last year only 27 per cent of registered architects were women.

The proportion of Māori graduates has also remained low, at between 9 and 22 per cent, the result, argues architectural historian Deidre Brown, of educational inequalities and subject availability at secondary schools, the financial burden of committing to a five-year degree, and a curriculum still dominated by Eurocentric thought and modes of learning. Nathu expands on this, describing the burden of communicating a non-Pākehā worldview for tutors and lecturers. Convincing a panel of critics or peers not only of your work but also of its relevance, she writes, 'is exhausting and discourages diversity in the work produced in architecture school'.

One of the obstacles identified by many of these writers is the lack of women role models for a new generation of young architects. As one interviewee says, 'You can't be what you can't see.' *Making Space* makes for essential reading for this new generation of architects. It's a serious read—a chapter by former *Urbis* editor Nicole Stock is a light and eloquent reprieve—but in asserting the presence and impact of women in architecture it provides a much-needed context for those early individuals who recognised the potential of architecture to meet the changing needs of communities far beyond the allure of a glossy photograph.

Soul-makers
Emma Gattey

My American Chair by Elizabeth Smither (Auckland University Press, 2022), 104pp, $24.99; **Renoir's Bicycle: A collection of prose poems** by Michael Harlow (Cold Hub Press, 2022), 80pp, $28

In 1985 Elizabeth Smither wrote that 'our individuality is best expressed when we focus on something outside or that we are most original when most absorbed'.[1] The poems in *My American Chair* are explorations of the outer and inner, seeking out both the tangible and intangible infrastructure of our lives.

Like Smither's titular American chair, the collection is cleaved in two, and is well balanced. Cherry and apple trees dance like young women through Part One, which opens with 'Cranes'. Evoking the precision of origami or ballet, Smither describes the 'choreography' and semaphore of the machines; she matches their nautical feel and their dance with her gratitude. Watching the construction of a casino from her hotel room, she muses:

> we have come this far
> we have built ourselves up by our own efforts
> we live here, thanks to cranes.

But is it ironic or in earnest? Is this really a celebration of construction, or a dirge for degrowth? There is plenty of ambiguity and duality throughout the book, with question marks hovering over several poems, and wryly acknowledged, 'for how could such a divided mouth / produce anything but ambiguity?' ('Your Top Lip').

Standalone, filmic vignettes, the poems are linked sequentially by shared words—almost codewords—that make the flow feel natural, unquestionable. They are also linked by themes: churches, angels, prayer, Catholicism, music, children, flowers, medicine, operations, hospitals, surgeons, and memorials. When these themes meld in one poem we get something like the purpose-bound organ music of 'In York Minster':

> Music is heart-height forever: it is
> its purpose and even the synod cannot
>   rescind it.
> Not the floor but not the heavens either.

Smither trucks with the leap and fertile *push* of life ('Overgrown Rockery'), as well as decay ('The Problem with Skeletons'). Planets swim in close pursuit of their suns; messy eaters chase drycleaning success from London to Paris; crowds save a duck from an incoming tram; children say a rueful 'reverse grace' while eating lambs' brains; we are invited to consider the form and function of white lies; Moomins make a cameo appearance. We could call this a smoke-and-mirrors book, if by smoke we mean representing, and by mirrors we mean lucid reflections of the everyday (the inherently miraculous). Smither offers a realism that feels magical.

Along with her often startling verb choices, Smither is unafraid of adjectives. They range from the purely descriptive ('green-glass', 'tired', 'concrete') to the abstractly evocative ('one mischievous spring'). A conjuror, she is deft. When we listen to a Soviet string quartet, it is beneath 'a lamp shaped like pantaloons', and we are *there*, before the 'little raised platform', in the seats 'fused together at the back'. These are the details that feel real, that make you feel you could have been there; indeed, *must* have been there—maybe we did/saw/dreamt this, too.

And when Smither adopts a child's eye and voice, it works. She is a child: practising pliés at 'the cut-throat barre'; cleaning up cat vomit; being praised for her swan-like neck, 'beauty unpromised, an unasked-for gift'. In 'Little Boy on the Lower Bunk', she speaks as one with sibling-filtered senses, one loved and led:

> I see the sky through a sister constellation.
> Always above me she admonishes me.
> I filter my sight through her advice.

When she creates charms and lullabies, it tugs heartstrings, it tugs at the unquantifiable. Chanting 'beautiful girl, beautiful girl'—the love-hymn of a grandmother—she recognises:

> I am bringing something I do not know
> down to you in my embrace. An angel's
> wingtip, the first air movement of
> a visitation of coming and forever grace.

This is love, mysterious and entire. And yet there is something more than love here. Jagged throughout the child-centred poems is a precocity, a sensuousness, a seepage of the adult world. Dolly Parton's lips and curves on a child's instrument ('The Euphonium'), a seven-year-old girl dieting all day for her birthday dinner, and undressing 'quicker than a catwalk model' ('Ruby's Seventh Birthday'; 'Ruby at Her Father's 47th Birthday'). This is the world as it plays, slightly off-kilter, in the life of a child. In relishing 'how pure it is', that 'first sleep-swathed morning kiss', Smither savours sweet intimacies, careful caresses, recording this unblemished love amidst the blemishes of the secular world ('Brushing a Child's Hair').

Occasionally, though, women feel—not maligned, exactly, but diminished. Their sphere of concern seems trivial. (Why must a planet's orbit be as close 'as a woman is to her handbag'?) Never the surgeon, always the receptionists in leopard-print, women are the butt of jokes. In 'The Joke of the Sapeurs-Pompiers', for example, the contrast is this: calm, wise male versus prideful, hysterical female. The punchline is female failure. And yes, we should be able to laugh at ourselves. And, to be fair, women are also honoured, written for, celebrated. In 'Poetry Reading with Women Poets' Smither conjures up 'a long-ago memory' with great love, solidarity, with the poets embracing despite sickness, and 'waving wildly, as if / it was something we owed to poetry: to hug / and kiss cheeks and sign ourselves for fever'. In 'Lucy at the Conference' the moral of the story is: women improve things, our platonic love performing some kind of alchemy that transforms lame events into 'a treat'.

One of the epigraphs opening *Renoir's Bicycle* is Christopher Middleton: 'A poem may be nourished by ideas but it has a life of its own.' Aptly, Michael Harlow does plenty of what he calls 'imagining forward' in these poems—taking an idea, a spark, and leaping energetically into its myriad possibilities. Love is usually the idea.

Brimming with nature, ekphrasis and life-writing, this collection recalls W.G. Sebald's prose poems in *After Nature*. He also brings to mind Billy Collins, Annie Dillard and Mary Oliver in his concise imagery and deep, soul-centred love of what we might call the cosmos. Like these writers, Harlow hears 'the song of poetry everywhere in the natural world' ('Mary Oliver, Poet'). But there is also a weirdness to these songs, a dark kind of grace. Some of Harlow's poems recall a David Lynch film: mindbending, freakish, uneasy-making dreams that tug at the seams of reality. His metier as Jungian therapist feeds this blurring between waking/dreaming, self/other, light/dark.

He constantly hears and sings love songs, love hymns, and usually the love poems and nature poems suggest dialogue. As with Smither's collection, there is a thick intertextuality within

Renoir's Bicycle: the poems reach out to one another, speak to one another. 'The holiness of attention' ends:

> All my thoughts speak of love.
> And who would want to silence any song.
> This is called the holiness of attention.

The middle line here speaks directly back to the preceding poem, and forward to many others. This bafflement, this non-rhetorical question, echoes throughout the collection: who would want to suppress the music of love/songs/poetry? Harlow speaks across and between anthologies to himself, to his readers, to the same (because infinite, because fundamental) subjects: nature as paramount, as life-giver, as vulnerable and as soul-maker; water as divining-rod, as bearer of truth; dreams as birthplace of poetry, as truth; the twinning of life and death. One of his crucial motifs is trees as 'very important people'. The final line of 'Curtain Raiser, Bach's Sinfonia in B flat' looks forward to 'The day Trees will become again very important people.' (This echoes the closing lines of 'All About the World'.) At this point, Harlow suggests we might be 'no longer strangers to ourselves'. We might see and hear the music, the truth, the profundity in what surrounds and shapes us.

Certain phrases snag like burrs in your mind, preserving light and space for when you next encounter them. The 'bronze key' and 'nailhead of light' catching a sleeve in 'Inexplicable Times' jolt our memory much later in the anthology. And 'the voices of unborn children' eerily whisper in 'Head Doctor' and 'Turning the Tables'. These missing children haunt many other poems.

Harlow ventriloquises, he honours, he brings to life: da Vinci, Sappho, Lincoln, Renoir, a legion of angels. (Not Cleopatra, only her 'astonishing breasts'.) Sappho looms large, and deliciously non-fragmentary. In 'The "Living Girl"' Sappho 'keeps turning up in my house of dreams', the girl who 'can't help but make / the music of love sing'. Her visitations are like creativity, like 'the way / a poem comes calling'. Unbidden, blissful, head over heels. The collection ends with Sappho, with insistence:

> All poems are about Love, you sing to the world.
> On the wings of words. Even when they aren't about
> Love. They are.
> ('All Poems, à Sappho')

The lust poems are frank, refreshing. There's a raunchy humour, intimations of 'what / went on in the cramped dark'. And suddenly a carnal moment—'When she touched him / there, they disappeared into each other'—fades out to the mundane: a blind fishmonger, begging. There is, too, in the love poems, a tenderness in minutiae: those touches of specific detail, of Flaubertian realism, that elevate a sex poem into a soulmate sex poem:

> Here, your same tortoise-shell spectacles propped

against the blue bowl of forget-me-nots;
　catching
the light of your Greek eyes ...

Here, like this, like this, and just now, like
　this.
('Here').

Harlow writes ekphrastic prose, illuminating works of art and music; he writes crisp, lyrical eulogies and morbid, magical realism that feels sinewy and dangerous; he writes the newsy, popular religion of late-night shows and American cable TV; he writes quote-heavy criminal case notes and occasionally dips his toes into theodicy, theorising the coexistence of a benevolent God and an evil world: 'that old question that is forever becoming / a new one ... Why does God have such clumsy hands?' He amplifies the voices of the unhinged: the unwell and the vaguely criminal, the insomniac and the hallucinatrix. There is something of the trickster in many of these poems: Pan, Puck, or perhaps a version of Sappho herself, playing japes from her love-couch.

Both Smither and Harlow love classical music as much as the healing music of grass, of nature. They love chairs, they love Abraham Lincoln ('Honest Abe'), angels, churches, secrets, truth, and they *love* love. Both are prolific writers (this is Smither's eighteenth book of poetry, Harlow's twelfth), and heavily laurelled. Dextrous, cunning and quick in their imagery, both are world-builders and myth-tellers. Both writers have sung to, for, and about each other in the past. For *Landfall* in 2014, Smither wrote that 'Harlow's mastery of the prose poem—almost his creation of it, for few other New Zealand poets come close—is an enduring legacy.'[2]

An earlier collection of Harlow's, *Vlaminck's Tie* (1985), contained a section of poems dedicated to Smither. Here, a dedication to Smither feels implicit, strongly so. In these latest collections, they could almost be writing *to* or *for* each other, with crossovers and shared thematic concerns, sharp artistic intelligence applied with concision, no rhyme, plenty of reason. You don't read Smither or Harlow—in these collections, at least—for scansion or metre. You read them for what Harlow has elsewhere called 'soul-making'.[3] Always a good reason to read a poem.

1　Elizabeth Smither, in Irihapeti Ramsden, Marian Evans and Miriama Evans (eds), *Wahine Kaituhi: Women writers of Aotearoa* (Spiral, 1985), 7.
2　Elizabeth Smither, 'What is it that Love Dares the Self to Do?,' Landfall Review Online, 1 June 2014: https://landfallreview.com/what-is-it-that-love-dares-the-self-to-do/
3　Michael Harlow, 'Making a Life in Central Otago' in Brian Turner, *Boundaries: People and places of Central Otago* (Penguin Random House, 2015), 178.

History Raw
Nicholas Reid

Voices from the New Zealand Wars | He Reo nō ngā Pakanga o Aotearoa by Vincent O'Malley (Bridget Williams Books, 2021), 440pp, $49.99

Vincent O'Malley has become our pre-eminent historian of the New Zealand Wars and their aftermath. He has already proven this in his *Beyond the Imperial Frontier: The contest for colonial New Zealand* (2014), *The Great War for New Zealand: Waikato 1800–2000* (2016) and *The New Zealand Wars | Ngā Pakanga o Aotearoa* (2019).

In each, he has provided a detailed and well-researched narrative, weighing evenly the perspectives of historical participants. But in *Voices from the New Zealand Wars* he does something different. Again, O'Malley's commentary presents a clear narrative of the New Zealand Wars, tracking from the Northern War of 1845–46 to the colonial power's conflict with Te Kooti, 1868–72. This time, however, it is the voices of the past that dominate.

By giving us the original writings and statements of 77 contemporary Māori and Pākehā, women and men, those who approved of the colonial enterprise and those who objected, O'Malley has transcended the dreaded historian's trap of 'presentism', whereby, anti-historically, the actions and thoughts of all people in the past are judged in terms of the values and priorities that we hold now.

We may now disapprove of some of the values expressed. We may flinch at the crude and racist language used in dispatches and memoirs (O'Malley does too; at one point he bowdlerises a racist slur such as 'n----r'). But we cannot deny that this is what those people thought and said. This is raw history, performed by the participants.

Inevitably, Pākehā voices dominate the earlier sections of this book. The first substantial Māori statement is Tāmihana Te Rauparaha's account of his father's final surrender and his time of peace and the building of the church in Ōtaki.

There are many different tones struck in these letters, memoirs, dispatches and verbatim replies to commissions. One thing is painfully clear: many of the colonial British officials and soldiers spoke or wrote with a degree of bad faith—that is, they knew that some of the policies they endorsed and promoted were deceptive and barely legal. To refer to iwi as 'rebels' was to assume that those opposed to invasion or the confiscation of land were breaking a contract, which was clearly not the case.

Writing to London, referring to the contentious Waitara purchase in Taranaki, Governor Gore Browne was unapologetic: 'I have insisted on this comparatively valueless purchase because if I had admitted the right of a Chief to interfere between me and the lawful proprietors of the soil, I should have found further acquisition of territory impossible in any part of New Zealand.' Translation: 'I am deliberately causing trouble so that I can set a precedent for grabbing land out from under the authority of rangatira.'

Many documents contain what can only be called self-serving bombast. In Taranaki, Lieutenant-Colonel Robert Carey's account of taking Mahoetahi is mainly written in deadpan journalese, but he begins by saying that iwi displayed 'their spirit of boastfulness and vaunting', and ends by claiming that 'The loss has been the greatest that Maori have ever suffered at the hands of Europeans, while no corresponding loss has been inflicted on us in return.' But, as O'Malley at once notes, this particular battle 'did not fundamentally alter the situation in Taranaki'. It was Lt-Col Carey himself who was displaying the 'boastfulness and vaunting'. There is similar vainglory when Sir George Grey boasts of his great victory in taking Weraroa Pā, when it was scarcely manned.

At Gate Pā (Pukehinahina) near Tauranga, British forces had the advantage of numbers and weapons and were over-confident about victory—which they did not achieve. Hōri Ngātai's account of this battle is the most vivid in the book, carefully noting strategy, how the rules of war were observed and the outcome. By contrast, Spencer Nicholl's account of the same engagement maintains a cocky tone, dismissive of the rules of war: 'I saw a lot of Maories coming across the open at the back of the Pah. If I had only had a rifle I could have knocked some of them over beautifully.'

There is the odd inadvertent or off-hand admission of massacres or atrocities carried out by colonial forces. O'Malley notes that the forest ranger Gustavus von Tempsky was no particular friend of the Māori people. But von Tempsky's account of the destruction of Rangiaowhia confirms that British forces knowingly torched a whare with people still in it.

To be sure, there were some Pākehā politicians, such as former Chief Justice Sir William Martin, who did genuinely protest at the invasion of Waikato and subsequent confiscation of land. Martin compared this with the Irish situation, predicting that confiscations in Waikato would create something like 'the brooding sense of wrong amongst the Irish, passed down from one generation to the next'.

This was an apt comparison in many ways. As O'Malley notes, Irish soldiers were over-represented in the British forces stationed in New Zealand and some Irish troopers made the same comparison. There were also colonial and British forces who showed real respect for the Māori they were fighting, marvelling and expressing admiration at Māori ingenuity and engineering skill in building fortifications. As often as not, such fortifications proved unassailable. General Cameron himself became sceptical of land-grabs and tired of fighting a war for land-hungry colonists.

Unfortunately the man who succeeded him, General Chute, had no such scruples and prosecuted the war brutally.

But as these documents show, many Pākehā politicians practised ambiguity. The most egregious example was Henry Sewell. He loudly protested against the confiscation of Māori land. *Voices From the New Zealand Wars* gives us six full pages of Sewell's cogent and impassioned arguments, saying confiscations benefitted only land speculators and politicians in Auckland. But, as O'Malley points out, as soon as Sewell became part of the next ministry, he suddenly changed his tune and defended such expropriation.

Māori responses (always presented to us bilingually) are usually calm and considered, most often found in petitions or pleas consciously addressing officials and people of power. In a long and eloquent letter to the provincial superintendent, James FitzGerald, Rēnata Kawepō argues point by point that the superintendent has forced war on Taranaki iwi, and then proceeds to shame FitzGerald by quoting biblical texts to support his claims. A committee in Ōpōtiki, addressing the Governor in Auckland, is even able to argue coolly that the killing, by Pai Mārire adherents, of the missionary Carl Volkner was justified in the light of the actions of British troops in Waikato. People of Poverty Bay petitioned not only about deprivation of land but the fact that many of them had been 'friendlies' who had fought against Pai Mārire and some of them were now being transported to the Chatham Islands.

Yet these documents also make it clear that not all Māori were of the same mind as the wars developed. The New Zealand Wars were not a simple story of racial conflict. Often iwi fought against tribal enemies or in pursuit of personal ambitions. Wiremu Tako Ngātata denounced the (Wakefield) New Zealand Company's claims to land in the central North Island, but still fought alongside colonial troops against Te Rangihaeta. In the East Coast wars around Tauranga, Te Arawa largely sided with colonial forces. On the west coast, a decisive battle on the small island of Moutoa was fought between Pai Mārire and 'friendlies'.

Most fractious was what O'Malley calls a 'civil war' among Ngāti Porou on the East Coast, where the iwi split into those who had embraced Pai Mārire and those who clung to Christianity, the latter becoming 'friendlies'. This is confirmed in the long narrative penned by Matuaera Nihoniho, who fought against Pai Mārire.

And in all this, there are some arresting voices of women. The first we encounter is that of Marianne Williams, wife of a missionary, whose language sounds a little quaint now. After Hōne Heke's sacking of Kororāreka she writes, 'God provided us help in our necessity. The tide of war has now rolled away from us in a season.' Much later, interrogated by a tribunal, Maata Morewarewa and Mereana Matau bear witness to colonial forces' attacks and killing of unarmed non-combatants. Later, Maraea Mōrete gives evidence against Te Kooti and his raids on outlying settlements and farms.

Here is so much hard contemporary evidence, and so many contemporary opinions expressed, that we do not merely discover facts about the past. We feel the nature of the past, its zeitgeist. At a time when we are urged to read and teach New Zealand history more thoroughly, this is obviously an essential text as well as being a work of great scholarship.

The book is generously illustrated with maps, photographs and contemporary artwork. Another way of bringing the past to life.

The Rhetoric of the Sixties
David Eggleton

Out of the Jaws of Wesley: 1944–1972 a record: Peter Olds selected and edited by Roger Hicken (Cold Hub Press, 2022), 112pp, $29.50

'I have my letter of resignation from society—my hair—my clothes—the material me which shines with praise and fades with the indifferences of [those] who choose not to understand anyway,' Peter Olds wrote in a letter to his parents in 1966 when he was 22, establishing this book's essential theme: the poet's early struggles to establish his own sense of identity and to realise his ambitions to be an artist in an indifferent or actively hostile society.

Peter Olds was born in 1944 into the Methodist Church. His father was a Methodist lay preacher and a beekeeper, and so was his grandfather. The family moved from Christchurch to Oxford to Milton to Dunedin, his father having become a full-time Methodist minister. In 1959, the family relocated to the Methodist parsonage in Herne Bay, Auckland. Olds found this shift to the bustling metropolis profoundly unsettling. Already rebellious through having been misdiagnosed at primary school as 'a slow learner', he dropped out of school at 16 and got work as an apprentice window-dresser in a menswear store on Queen Street. Running with the wrong crowd, he became a bodgie and eventually a juvenile delinquent, converting cars and taking them for thrill rides, ending up 'in clink and detention centre'.

Olds also became possessor of a clapped-out 1939 Ford V8 coup to hoon around in. Lying under this vehicle while repairing the engine resulted in a major injury and the loss of sight in his left eye.

In 1965, at the age of 20, Olds moved back to Dunedin, as if back to his roots, but later in the year returned to Auckland, beginning a long period of restless toing and froing between the two cities. During this time, he was writing, though at first, under the influence of the era's ferment of popular music, he tried to write songs.

Out of the Jaws of Wesley is not a formal memoir but a scrapbook, put together by publisher and friend Roger Hickin and assembled out of hand-written letters, pen-and-pencil drawings, battered snapshots, press cuttings, many unpublished prose vignettes, and excerpts from published poems. In a way, it's a collage of a now mythic era, redolent with echoes of the rhetoric of the Sixties.

From mendicant mystics, to destitution as a sign of sanctity, to suffering as a beatitude and a path to spiritual enlightenment, the symbolic rites of passage are here. From existentialism in the manner of Albert Camus and exhortations to keep moving on in the manner of Jack Kerouac, to Jimi Hendrix, James K. Baxter and William Blake, the tropes of the youth revolution as it played out in New Zealand are presented with granular fidelity, through the poet's meticulous attention to language.

On the cover, an impish young Peter Olds is shown, like James Dean or Marlon Brando, as one of the wild ones, a cigarette dangling from the side of his mouth. Next to that photo is a latter-day image showing him much older and rueful—as if weathered by many psychic storms. In his previous book *Sheep Truck and Other Poems*, Olds wrote what he called his 'last poem'. Since then, he has retreated into silence.

Rimbaud reckoned the poet must become a seer 'by a long, gigantic and rational derangement of the senses'. Olds, along with many of his generation, sought the visionary through drugs, but as he writes here: 'I took too much surrealism & wound up in the bin.'

One might see this book as survivor literature. Certainly, it is no misery memoir; rather, it reveals Olds's beginnings as a street poet with an observational gift for the absurdist comedy of the everyday. Amongst the outcasts, the marginalised, the so-called dregs of society, Olds searches, in a spirit of enquiry and with an almost religious sense of vocation, to craft poems that respond to the human condition as he experiences it.

The former lunatic asylums or psychiatric hospitals at Seacliff and Cherry Farm cast titanic shadows in those days. They loomed, forbidding and Gothic, as institutions almost the size of small towns. Those who tried to abscond sometimes drowned in the Waikouaiti River; others were slugged with ECT or pills. The authorities swooped on misfits and cast them into the looney bin on an industrial scale. Olds describes the travails of his own recreational pill-popping as a kind of closed circuit, in and out of 'treatment', when barbiturates were seen as a panacea for all manner of ills.

As a proto-beatnik in the early 1960s, Olds mooches 'from coffee bar to coffee bar' in Wellington and locates a carnivalesque demi-monde of Dickensian grotesques. It's a world he only briefly sketches, but it's also a transgressive world that has vanished. Later in the decade, hippies and mass protest movements would help bring about the cultural turn towards therapy and diversity.

As part of the hippie trail between Auckland and Dunedin, Olds establishes a crash-pad at a house on Montgomery Avenue by the Leith River in Dunedin (attempts to catch eels go awry), which 'the infamous and the notorious' visit, and which the drug squad raids, but ultimately he is less interested in being a Christ-like salvationist for acid casualties than he is in becoming a writer true to himself.

He travels to Christchurch to try and get a book of poems published by Caxton Press or Albion Press, but the publishers are dismissive and condescending. Yet Charles Brasch and James K. Baxter are amongst those who wrote verse letters to Olds. This miscellany ends in 1972 when a new publisher, Trevor Reeves of Caveman Press in Dunedin, enthusiastically champions Olds and publishes his first collection *Lady Moss Revived*. The following year, Olds was included in the landmark *The Young New Zealand Poets*, edited by Arthur Baysting, which also featured Sam Hunt, Ian Wedde, Alan Brunton and Bill Manhire. Peter Olds had emphatically arrived as a poet, an important voice for his life and times.

New from Te Herenga Waka University Press

Birnam Wood, a novel by Eleanor Catton
A Lack of Good Sons, poetry by Jake Arthur
Selected Poems, by Andrew Johnston
Past Lives, poetry by Leah Dodd
Ruin, short stories by Emma Hislop
Ithaca, essays by Alie Benge
This Is a Story About Your Mother, poetry by Louise Wallace
Calamities!, poetry by Jane Arthur
Dream Girl, short stories by Joy Holley
The Artist, poetry by Ruby Solly
Pet, a novel by Catherine Chidgey
Honouring Our Ancestors: Takatāpui, Two-Spirit and Indigenous LGBTQI+ Well-being, edited by Alison Green and Leonie Pihama
As the Trees Have Grown, poetry by Stephanie de Montalk
The Selected Poems, by James K. Baxter, edited by John Weir

TE HERENGA WAKA
UNIVERSITY PRESS
VICTORIA UNIVERSITY OF WELLINGTON

The world awaits...

Our pop-up travel bookshop is open now!

NEXT DOOR

03 379 2882   scorpiobooks.co.nz

NEW FROM OTAGO UNIVERSITY PRESS

Katherine Mansfield's Europe
Station to Station
by Redmer Yska
ISBN 9781990048531
Jacketed paperback, $50

Respirator
A Poet Laureate Collection 2019–2022
by David Eggleton
ISBN 9781990048500
Hardback, $35

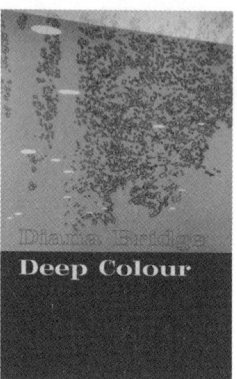

Deep Colour
by Diana Bridge
ISBN 9781990048548
Paperback, $25

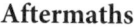

Aftermaths
Colonialism, Violence and Memory in Australia, New Zealand and the Pacific
Edited by Angela Wanhalla, Lyndall Ryan and Camille Nurka
ISBN 9781990048449
Paperback, $50

OTAGO UNIVERSITY PRESS
Find our books in all good bookstores
Visit us at oup.nz

CASELBERG TRUST INTERNATIONAL poetry PRIZE 2023

Supported by

FIRST PRIZE: $500
+ one week stay at the Caselberg House, Broad Bay, Dunedin

SECOND PRIZE: $250

HIGHLY COMMENDED
(no monetary prize)

2023 judge: **RHIAN GALLAGHER**
ENTRIES OPEN: **1 June 2023**
ENTRIES CLOSE: **31 July 2023**

The first and second placed poems will be published in the November 2023 edition of Landfall

For Conditions & Entry Form:
www.caselbergtrust.org

CASELBERG Trust

The Landfall Essay Competition 2023

THE LANDFALL ESSAY COMPETITION seeks to encourage Aotearoa writers to continue the tradition of vivid, contentious and creative essay writing.

ENTRIES will be judged by *Landfall* editor Lynley Edmeades and the winner will receive $3000 and a year's subscription to *Landfall*. The winning essay will be published in *Landfall 246*. Entries also have the chance of publication in *Strong Words 4: The best of the Landfall Essay Competition*.

RECENT COMPETITION WINNERS INCLUDE Tina Makereti, Andrew Dean, A.M. McKinnon, Tobias Buck, Nina Mingya Powles, Alice Miller, Laurence Fearnley, Alie Benge, Airini Beautrais and Tracey Slaughter.

SUBMISSIONS CLOSE JULY 31

OTAGO UNIVERSITY PRESS
Te Whare Tā o Te Wānanga o Ōtākou
oup.nz

For more information go to:
oup.nz/landfall-essay-comp

UNIVERSITY BOOK SHOP

For all booklovers, *everywhere.*

Visit us soon in our newly refurbished store

378 Great King Street, Dunedin | Open 7 Days
Ph 03 477 6976 | unibooks.co.nz

The **Kathleen Grattan Award for Poetry** 2023

PRIZE: $10,000 CASH AND A PUBLISHING CONTRACT

JUDGE: ANNE KENNEDY

ENTRIES CLOSE 31 JULY 2023

Entry details at
oup.nz/kathleen-grattan-award

 OTAGO UNIVERSITY PRESS

LF Young Writers' Essay Competition 2024

PRIZE: $500 + A YEAR'S SUBSCRIPTION TO LANDFALL

JUDGE: LYNLEY EDMEADES

ENTRIES CLOSE 31 MARCH 2024

Entry details at
oup.nz/yw-essay-comp

 OTAGO UNIVERSITY PRESS

CONTRIBUTORS

Philip Armstrong's *Sinking Lessons* (OUP, 2020) won the Kathleen Grattan Poetry Award in 2019. His recent poems have appeared in *Landfall*, *Poetry New Zealand Yearbook*, *PN Review* and *Pleiades*.

Nick Ascroft's latest poetry collection, *The Stupefying* (THWUP, 2022), is still in the shops if you hurry. Victor Billot in *Landfall Review Online* says it is 'like a galactic nebula, brightly lit and sparkling with colour'. It isn't at all, though.

Rebecca Ball is a teacher from Ōtautahi, New Zealand. She has published writing in journals and anthologies, including *Landfall*, *London Grip*, *Turbine|Kapohau* and *Poetry New Zealand Yearbook*.

Airini Beautrais is a writer and teacher based in Whanganui. She is working on a collection of essays on personal, political and spiritual themes.

Holly Best is an artist and writer based in Ōtautahi Christchurch. She is studying towards a Master of Writing at Canterbury University.

Sally Blundell is a freelance journalist, writer and reviewer in Ōtautahi Christchurch. She was the books and culture editor for the *NZ Listener* and a judge in the 2018 Ockham New Zealand Book Awards (fiction category) and the 2021 New Zealand Heritage Literary Awards (non-fiction). Her book on the new Ravenscar House in Christchurch, *Ravenscar House: A biography*, was published by CUP in 2022.

Ahimsa Timoteo Bodhrán is the author of *Archipiélagos*, *Antes y después del Bronx: Lenapehoking*, and *South Bronx Breathing Lessons*, and editor of *Yellow Medicine Review*'s queer Indigenous and *Movement Research Performance Journal*'s Native issues. His work in Aotearoa is in *Bravado*, *Brief*, *Catalyst*, *Enamel*, *Landfall* and *Poetry New Zealand*.

Cindy Botha lives in Tauranga, where she began writing after six decades of doing other things. She has been published in New Zealand, the UK and the USA.

Liz Breslin writes poems and stories, including *In Bed with the Feminists* (Dead Bird Books, 2021) and *Alzheimer's and a Spoon* (OUP, 2017, 2021).

Medb Charleton is originally from Ireland. Her poetry has appeared in *Landfall*, *Sport* and *Poetry New Zealand*, among others. She recently started a PhD at the University of Waikato.

Janet Charman's collection, *The Pistils* (OUP, 2022), was longlisted for the Mary and Peter Biggs Poetry Prize at the 2023 Ockham New Zealand Book Awards. Her monograph 'Smoking! The Homoerotic Subtext of *Man Alone* – A Matrixial Reading', is forthcoming from Steele Roberts.

Jennifer Compton was born in Wellington but now lives in Melbourne.

She is a poet and playwright who also writes prose.

Brett Cross lives in the Waikato, where he runs two small publishing presses. He has previously published work in several journals, including *Cordite*, *Poetry New Zealand* and *Brief*.

Jodie Dalgleish is a writer, curator and sound artist based in Luxembourg. Her poetry has been published in *Landfall*, *Poetry Aotearoa New Zealand Yearbook 2023*, *Shearsman*, *The Long Poem Magazine*, *Poetry Salzburg Review*, *Azure* and *Les Cahiers Luxembourgeois*. She holds a Master of Creative Writing from AUT.

Jackie Davis lives in Palmerston North. She holds an MA in Creative Writing and is the author of two novels published by Penguin Books NZ. She has been published in New Zealand, Australia, Japan, the US and the UK, and she continues to write to find herself.

Mark Edgecombe lives in Tawa with Sarah and their children William, Elise and Bethany. Poems of his have appeared in *Landfall*, *takahē*, *Meniscus* and *Quadrant*.

Jonny Edwards is an English teacher in Whangārei. He was born in Christchurch and formerly worked as a journalist there and in Otago.

David Eggleton is a writer and poet based in Ōtepoti Dunedin. His latest collection of poems is *Respirator: A Poet Laureate Collection 2019–2022* (OUP, 2023).

Chris Else is a writer, reviewer and manuscript assessor. He lives in Dunedin.

Shirley Eng writes short stories and poetry. She has been published in New Zealand Poetry Society publications and *takahē*. She was long-listed in the John O'Connor First Book Award 2022 for Best First Book of Poetry.

Alexandra Fraser has published work in magazines and anthologies in New Zealand and overseas. She has two collections of poetry published by Steele Roberts: *Conversation by Owl Light* and *Startrails*.

Amber French grew up in Waitakaruru, Hauraki Plains. She lives in Auckland now and writes poetry. Amber is a university library assistant.

Emma Gattey is a writer and critic from Ōtautahi. She is working on a PhD in New Zealand history at the University of Cambridge and is a Research Fellow for Te Takarangi at the University of Otago Faculty of Law.

Tim Grgec's first book, *All Tito's Children*, was published by THWUP in 2021 and featured in the *NZ Listener*'s 10 best poetry collections. The IIML included the book's concluding poem, 'Lyall Bay, 1959' in the 2021 edition of *Ōrongohau|Best New Zealand Poems*.

Danielle Heyhoe is a writer who lives in Aotearoa with her husband and three sons. Her fiction has been published in *takahē* and *Headland*, and through Penguin and Something Other Press, Paris. She was shortlisted for the Sargeson Prize 2020.

Gavin Hipkins is an award-winning Tāmaki Makaurau-based artist. He has exhibited widely over the last three decades. He is an Associate Professor at Te Waka Tūhura Elam School of Fine Arts and Design, the University of Auckland.

Lincoln Jaques holds a Master of Creative Writing. His poetry, fiction and travel essays have appeared in Aotearoa and internationally. He was runner-up in the 2022 IWW Kathleen Grattan Prize for a Sequence of Poems.

Paula King lives and works in Manawatū. In 2016 she completed a Master of Creative Writing at the IIML. Her poems can be found in *Turbine|Kapohau*, *PoetryNZ*, *Swamp*, *FlashFrontier*, the *takahē* poetry prize 2014, and *the unexpected greenness of trees* (poems from the Caselberg Trust). Her poem 'too much telling' was highly commended in the Caselberg Poetry Prize 2022.

Brent Kininmont's poems can be found online, in previous issues of *Landfall*, and in his collection *Thuds Underneath* (THWUP, 2016).

Jackson McCarthy is a poet and student from Auckland currently studying in Wellington. He was a finalist for the Schools Poetry Award 2021. His work has been published in *Tarot*, *Starling*, *Landfall* and elsewhere.

Maria McMillan was raised in Ōtautahi Christchurch and lives on the Kāpiti Coast. She has published a poetry sequence, *The Rope Walk* (Seraph Press, 2013), and two full-length collections: *Tree Space* (VUP, 2014) and *The Ski Flier* (VUP, 2017).

Zoë Meager's work has appeared in *Cheap Pop*, *Ellipsis Zine*, *Granta*, *Hue and Cry*, *Landfall*, *Lost Balloon*, *Mascara Literary Review*, *Mayhem*, *Meniscus*, *North & South*, *Overland*, *Splonk*, and *Turbine|Kapohau*, among others.

Michael Mintrom is a New Zealander who lives in Melbourne, Australia. His poetry has appeared previously in many literary journals, including *Landfall*, *Sport*, *takahē*, *Cordite*, *Meanjin* and *Westerly*.

Ruben Mita is a musician and writer living in Pōneke, trying to connect words, sounds, plants and people. His camera roll consists solely of photos of fungi.

Josiah Morgan (Kāi Tahu, Ngāti Maniapoto) is a multimedia artist living in Ōtautahi Christchurch. He is the author of four books, most recently *Road: A Postlapsarian Comedy* (Feral Dove, 2022).

Emma Neale has had six novels, six collections of poetry, and one book of short fiction published. She is the mother of two sons and lives in Dunedin, where she works as a freelance editor.

Bill Nelson's first poetry collection, *Memorandum of Understanding*, was published in 2016. He lives and works in Wellington and has a verse novel forthcoming from THWUP.

Gregory O'Brien's most recent book, *House and Contents*, is a collection of poems and paintings. His monograph about artist Don Binney is forthcoming from AUP in 2023.

Annabelle O'Meara has lived in the Wellington-Wairarapa area for the past 20 years. She celebrated turning 70 in 2022 by opening an Instagram account in a personal challenge to write more poems.

Lisa Onland recently returned to New Zealand after over a decade living abroad. Her short fiction has been published in *takahē*, and she is working on her first novel. Lisa lives in Wellington with her young family.

Claire Orchard's work has appeared in various journals and anthologies. Her first poetry collection, *Cold Water Cure*, was published by VUP in 2016.

James Pasley is a writer from Auckland. He has an MA from the IIML. His writing has appeared in *Landfall, Newsroom, The Spinoff's The Sunday Essay, takahē* and *Turbine|Kapohau*. His short story 'Teetering' was runner-up for the 2022 Sunday Star Times Short Story award.

Lorenz Poeschl (Pöschl) is a researcher and academic-English teacher from Auckland. His work touches on colonialism, pedagogy, national memory and intimacy. As a German immigrant to Aotearoa, Lorenz writes to think about strangeness in a settler-colonial territory. His writing has appeared in zines, *Write Together* and the *Journal of New Zealand Literature*.

Jenny Powell is a secondary school teacher and the Dunedin UNESCO City of Literature South D Poet Lorikeet. Her latest poetry collection, *Meeting Rita*, was published by Cold Hub Press in 2021.

Nafanua Purcell Kersel is a Sāmoan poet, performer and writer raised in Aotearoa and based in Te Matau-a-Māui. Her poetry is published in *Vines, Vā: Stories by women of the moana* and *Turbine|Kapohau*. She has recently completed an MA in Creative Writing from IIML.

Brett Reid lives in Auckland Tāmaki Makaurau. When he's not swimming or cycling, he's walking slowly toward the challenge of his first collection, hopeful he gets there before the only deadline that really matters.

Nicholas Reid's doctorate is in history. He convened the General Non-Fiction panel of the 2022 Ockham New Zealand Book Awards and, together with fellow judges Aaron Smale and Leilani Tamu, selected from 56 entries Vincent O'Malley's *Voices from the New Zealand Wars | He Reo nō ngā Pakanga o Aotearoa* for the 2022 General Non-Fiction Award. His review is exclusively his own opinion and does not necessarily represent those of Smale or Tamu.

Evangeline Riddiford Graham is the author of poetry chapbooks *La Belle Dame avec les Mains Vertes* (Compound Press) and *Ginesthoi* (hard press). Her poetry can also be found in *Sweet Mammalian*, *The Spinoff* and *Westerly*. Recent art exhibitions include *nature danger revenge* (Dunedin Public Art Gallery) and *wax tablet* (Te Tuhi). She is the creator and host of poetry podcast Multi-Verse.

Amanda Shanley is a ceramicist who specialises in useful mugs, plates and bowls, each a unique creation and sometimes a little off kilter. Her studio and gallery are in the heart of the creative Ōtepoti, her adopted home of 25 years.

Derek Schulz is an award-winning poet, essayist and writer of fiction. He won the Caselberg IPP in 2018, was runner-up in 2019 and shortlisted again in 2021. Recent essays have featured in *Landfall*, *Strong Words* (OUP, 2019, 2021), *Poetry New Zealand Yearbook 2021* and *The Spinoff*. His fiction has appeared in the *NZ Listener*, *Landfall* and *Sport*.

Kerrin P. Sharpe has published four collections of poetry (all with THWUP). She has also had poems published in NZ and overseas, including *Landfall*, *Oxford Poets 13* (Carcanet Press), *Blackbox Manifold*, *Poetry* (USA), *PN Review* (UK) and *Stand* (UK). 'Te hau o te atau/the breath of heaven' was written with the assistance of an arts continuity grant provided by Creative New Zealand in 2020.

Anya Sinclair lives in Ōtepoti Dunedin. She has a BFA (Elam/Dunedin School of Art) and has had solo exhibitions at Tauranga Art Gallery and Ashburton Art Gallery.

Rachel Smith writes in Ōtautahi Christchurch. She has been published in journals and anthologies, including *Landfall*, *Best Small Fictions 2020* and *Best Microfiction 2019*. She was a recipient of the NZSA Complete MS Manuscript assessment in 2021 and is an editor at Flash Frontier. She is screenwriter for the feature film, *Stranded Pearl*, released in February 2023.

Rachael Taylor is a writer and artist living in Ōtautahi Christchurch. Her work has appeared in *Landfall*, *Flash Frontier* and *takahē*.

Nicola Thorstensen is a student of Massey University's creative writing programme. Her work has appeared in New Zealand publications, including *takahē*, *Poetry New Zealand*, *Landfall* and the political anthology *Manifesto Aotearoa*.

Steven Toussaint was born and raised in Chicago. After graduating from the Iowa Writers' Workshop, he moved to New Zealand in 2011. He now lives with his wife and daughter in Cambridge, England. His books include *The Bellfounder* (The Cultural Society, 2015) and *Lay Studies* (VUP, 2019), which was shortlisted for the Mary and Peter Biggs Poetry Prize at the 2020 Ockham New Zealand Book Awards. You can find more of his work in *Image*, *The Spinoff*, *The Winter Anthology*, POETRY and *Commonweal*.

Tim Upperton's third poetry collection is *A Riderless Horse* (AUP, 2022). He lives in Palmerston North.

Nicholas Wright teaches literature and creative writing at Te Whare Wānanga o Waitaha, Ōtautahi. His poetry has appeared in *Landfall*, *Otoliths*, *The Spinoff*, and *Poetry New Zealand Yearbook*. He is currently writing a book of essays on poetry in Aotearoa.

Phoebe Wright grew up in Ōtautahi Christchurch and is now based in Te Whanganui-a-tara Wellington. She is a writer of fiction and poetry and is working on a novel.

Xiaole Zhan is a writer and composer. They were the winner of the National Schools Poetry Award 2019 and the first-equal winner of the 2019 Secondary Schools Division of the Sargeson Short Story Prize.

CONTRIBUTIONS

Landfall publishes original poems, essays, short stories, excerpts from works of fiction and non-fiction in progress, reviews, articles on the arts, and portfolios by artists. Submissions must be emailed to landfall@otago.ac.nz with 'Landfall submission' in the subject line.

For further information visit our website oup.nz/landfall

SUBSCRIPTIONS

Landfall is published in May and November. The subscription rates for 2023 (two issues) are: New Zealand $55 (including GST); Australia $NZ65; rest of the world $NZ70. Sustaining subscriptions help to support New Zealand's longest running journal of arts and letters, and the writers and artists it showcases. These are in two categories: Friend: between $NZ75 and $NZ125 per year. Patron: $NZ250 and above.

Send subscriptions to Otago University Press, PO Box 56, Dunedin, New Zealand. For enquiries, email landfall@otago.ac.nz or call 64 3 479 8807.

Print ISBN: 978-1-99-004855-5
ePDF ISBN: 978-1-99-004865-4
ISSN 00–23–7930

Copyright © Otago University Press 2023

Published by Otago University Press
533 Castle Street, Dunedin
New Zealand

Typeset by Otago University Press.
Printed in New Zealand by Caxton.

Amanda Shanley, *Large Pencil Bowl*, Primo Production White Earthenware clay. Coloured with underglaze crayons and clear glaze, 130 x 200mm. Image courtesy of the artist.